NO CHILD IS UNADOPTABLE

SAGE HUMAN SERVICES GUIDES, VOLUME 8

Sage Human Services Guides

a series of books edited by ARMAND LAUFFER and published in cooperation with the Continuing Education Program in the Human Services of the University of Michigan School of Social Work

---

Volume 1: **GRANTSMANSHIP**
by Armand Lauffer with contributions by Milan Dluhy, William Lawrence, and Eloise Snyder

Volume 2: **CREATING GROUPS**
by Harvey J. Bertcher and Frank F. Maple

Volume 3: **UNDERSTANDING YOUR SOCIAL AGENCY**
by Armand Lauffer, Lynn Nybell, Carla Overberger, Beth Reed, and Lawrence Zeff

Volume 4: **SHARED DECISION MAKING**
by Frank F. Maple

Volume 5: **VOLUNTEERS**
by Armand Lauffer and Sarah Gorodezky with contributions by Jay Callahan and Carla Overberger

Volume 6: **RESOURCES: For Child Placement and Other Human Services**
by Armand Lauffer with contributions by Bonnie Carlson, Kayla Conrad, and Lynn Nybell

Volume 7: **FINDING FAMILIES: An Ecological Approach to Family Assessment in Adoption**
by Ann Hartman

Volume 8: **NO CHILD IS UNADOPTABLE: A Reader on Adoption of Children with Special Needs**
by Sallie R. Churchill, Bonnie Carlson, and Lynn Nybell

Volume 9: **HEALTH NEEDS OF CHILDREN**
by Roger Manela and Armand Lauffer with contributions by Eugene Feingold and Ruben Meyer

NO CHILD IS UNADOPTABLE

A Reader on Adoption of
Children with Special Needs

A Project CRAFT Publication
Edited by Sallie R. Churchill,
Bonnie Carlson, and Lynn Nybell

Volume 8
SAGE HUMAN SERVICES GUIDES

Published in cooperation with
- The North American Center on Adoption, Inc. and
- The Continuing Education Program in the Human Services of the University of Michigan School of Social Work

CRAFT = Curriculum Resources for Adoption and
Foster Care Training

SAGE PUBLICATIONS Beverly Hills/London

For information address:

SAGE PUBLICATIONS, INC.
275 South Beverly Drive
Beverly Hills, California 90212

SAGE PUBLICATIONS LTD
28 Banner Street
London ECIY 8QE

Printed in the United States of America

Library of Congress Cataloging in Publication Data

Main entry under title:

No child is unadoptable.

(Sage human services guides ; v. 8)
Includes bibliographical references.
1. Adoption—United States 2. Special needs children
3. Problem children I. Churchill, Sallie R. II. Carlson, Bonnie.
III. Nybell, Lynn.
HV875.N55 362.7'34 78-26357
ISBN 0-8039-1215-3 pbk.

FIRST PRINTING

CONTENTS

INTRODUCTION

We owe a debt to four social workers for their efforts in developing this reader. Robin Aronow, Sally Bielema, Beverly Curtin, and Pamela Dilley reviewed and criticized over three hundred articles from the practitioner's point of view. We used their opinions to guide our selection of articles for this book. All four have received MSWs from the University of Michigan.

This manuscript was edited by Ellen Saalberg and typed by Victoria Decker. We appreciate their cheerful and professional work.

Together with its two companion monographs, this guide is the product of an ongoing training project conducted at the University of Michigan School of Social Work. Aimed at developing leaders in adoption and foster care practices, Project CRAFT (Curriculum Resources in Adoption and Foster Care Training) was initially supported by a grant of the Edna McConnell Clark Foundation. Its sponsorship has expanded to include federal, state, and local agencies. Project CRAFT owes much to the continuing encouragement of the Clark Foundation's executive vice-president, Peter Forsythe.

Sallie R. Churchill, Bonnie Carlson, and Lynn Nybell

Ann Arbor, 1979

ABOUT THIS BOOK

No Child Is Unadoptable is Volume 8 of the *Sage Human Services Guides* published by Sage Publications, and developed by the Continuing Education Program in the Human Services of the University of Michigan School of Social Work. Professor Armand Lauffer is Series Editor.

The following guides were developed by the staff of Project CRAFT (Curriculum Resources for Adoption and Foster Care Training):

Resources: For Child Placement and Other Human Services by Armand Lauffer with contributions by Bonnie Carlson, Kayla Conrad, and Lynn Nybell (Volume 6, SHSG)

Finding Families: An Ecological Approach to Family Assessment in Adoption by Ann Hartman (Volume 7, SHSG)

No Child Is Unadoptable: A Reader on Adoption of Children with Special Needs edited by Sallie R.. Churchill, Bonnie Carlson, and Lynn Nybell (Volume 8, SHSG)

Work on these guides was funded through a grant by the Edna McConnell Clark Foundation. The concepts in each were tested with seasoned practitioners and administrators from child welfare agencies throughout the United States and Canada. A subsequent grant from the Children's Bureau, U.S. Department of Health, Education and Welfare, facilitated the dissemination of these materials.

Section I

INTRODUCTION TO A NEW KIND OF ADOPTION

In the mid-1950s a young couple unable to become biological parents sought to adopt a child. Having met the adoption agency's rather inscrutable criteria, they were allowed to accept twins into their home. They expected to pass "the test of parenting" and to have the adoption finalized within a year, but all was not well. While one twin developed normally over the next few months, the other developed mild cerebral palsy.

The parents loved both children dearly and wanted to adopt both. The agency acknowledged that the couple made fine parents and they could provide adequately for the twins. However, it recommended the final adoption of the child who had developed normally, but did not recommend the adoption of the child with cerebral palsy. The reason—could people be good parents if they wanted a defective child?

This was not an isolated experience; it represents a conflict between two perspectives on adoption. We think it helpful to give these two kinds of adoption different titles—Adoption I and Adoption II. We define these terms in the following way:

Adoption I: furnishing a service to childless couples that gives them an opportunity to raise a child from infancy and to substitute as closely as possible for biological parents, as well as fulfilling a nurturing parental role.

Adoption II: furnishing a service to children deeply in need of a parent or parents who can provide them with nurturing despite atypical patterns of needs and responses, their older ages, or their minority or mixed biological heritages.

We chose the terms Adoption I and Adoption II because they are neutral. By using these terms, we hope to help the reader make the nonjudgmental but important differentiation spelled out above. Our review of the literature shows that this differentiation had not been made systematically by all authors. Some authors use cumbersome phrases such as "adoption for the hard to place child," or "adoption for the child who is special." These phrases are imprecise and limiting. In addition, some descriptions of how Adoption II differs from Adoption I have been defensive or negative.

Both Adoption I and Adoption II are social institutions providing critical services for human beings in need. They are both dedicated to finding and maintaining permanency for family members. Recently the availability of birth control, the legalization of abortion, and changes in the social climate that permit unmarried mothers the opportunity to keep their own children without social ostracism, have greatly reduced the number of children available for Adoption I. At the same time, changing social attitudes, medical improvements, and adoption law changes have made possible the increased use of Adoption II.

This book of readings is about Adoption II, the adoption of children once labeled "hard to place." Authors in this book give evidence of deep commitments to children who are very needful of parents and of permanency, despite handicaps that have previously been considered deterrents to adoption. It is about a commitment to parenting that emphasizes the great capacity of adults to assume a nurturing parent role when given the opportunity, appropriate financial aid, and counseling.

Finally, the book is about the commitment of adoption workers, community workers, and legislators who have been willing to challenge the status quo—the prejudice in legislative chambers, social agencies, and local communities. The authors of each article describe the development of Adoption II, an incredible and seemingly impossible implementation of an ideal turned into an increasingly available reality.

We have tried to present an overview of the work done to assure that children with special needs will be adopted. We have drawn from literature based on research, professional experience, ideological stands, and real family experiences.

Our intention is to provide the reader with a broad understanding of the problems involved in Adoption II. We introduce some of the current solutions to those problems. Most important, we hope the book will result in strong commitments to the development of more successful and creative efforts in the placement of children who should no longer be defined as "hard to place."

An overview of the issues around Adoption II is presented in Section 1 where we begin with a speech by Graeme Gregory. Gregory speaks of the revolution in adoption that has taken place in the United States. Painting a warm, historical picture of the changes that have permitted the growth of Adoption II, he shows how Adoption II meets children's needs when workers tap into the nurturing capacity of adults.

The articles in Section 2 address the changing concepts: "Who is the adoptable child? Who is the adoptive family?" Several articles deal with the unique aspects of finding homes for children previously called hard to place—black children, adolescents, children with mental retardation. Other articles in Section 2 explore the nature of suitable adoptive families, including single parents. The section ends with a sensitive report from the firing line, an account of one adoptive family's experience called *The Gift of Love.*

Section 3 covers the special tasks that are so necessary to make Adoption II work, including selecting the child and family for each other and preparing them for adoption. We conclude with a frank look at the event of disruption of adoption placements.

Section 4 explores a few of the new programs developed to facilitate the successful practice of Adoption II.

1

NO CHILD IS UNADOPTABLE

GRAEME GREGORY

In this speech, Gregory introduces his Australian audience to the history and principles of Adoption II. As he does so he captures for us much of what is at the heart of this revolution in adoption practice.

THE CHILDREN WHO WAIT

Tracey is six months old and has Down's Syndrome, more commonly called Mongoloidism. She has not achieved any developmental milestone, and does not support her head very well. She is a contented baby, who will eagerly display her beautiful smile for all to see.

Jean is happy, bubbly and very cute twelve-month-old. She is good natured and at this time she seems to be within the average range of development. Jean was born with a congenital absence of her left eye and a cataract which has caused almost total blindness in her right eye. She can, however, distinguish between light and dark.

Robert, nine-and-a-half, and Paul, eleven, are brothers. Paul has experienced much rejection in the past, and is quite an angry and aggressive boy as a result. He does well in school. In his former foster home, Robert was the favorite and Paul knew it. When Paul returned home last summer after attending camp, his foster mother requested his

Editors' Note: Adapted from an address to the general meeting, Children's Welfare Association of Victoria, Australia, October 27, 1972. By Graeme Gregory, B.A., Dip. Soc. Stud., M.S.W.

removal. He is not in a new foster home. Paul puts up a "front" when you first meet him. He sort of has a "shield" around himself which he probably uses in order to protect himself from further rejection, as in the past. Robert is the more quiet, friendly and polite of the two. He is a slow learner, but retains everything. Just recently Robert was placed in the same home with his brother. This was quite a happy reunion, since they had a good relationship as brothers.

These short histories of children could be typical of those children in many institutions or foster placements. These come from a list of children awaiting adoption in Massachusetts. The full expectation of the adoption workers responsible for these children is that they will find permanent homes with adoptive parents.

That is part of the tremendous revolution that has occurred in the adoption scene in recent years in the United States. Children who ten years ago would be considered unadoptable are being adopted. And married couples, and single people, who ten years ago would be considered unsuitable as adoptive parents, are adopting children. I do not think this revolution has come through in its full extent in the literature. My exposure to it has challenged almost every precept I have formerly held about adoption practice, and I have been forced to rethink my own position on adoption. But even more, I have been forced to rethink again about the needs of children. And I have come to the conclusion that in adoption practice we do not primarily at all times think first of the needs of the child. Instead we think of the needs of adoptive parents and their limitations, and in doing so condemn hundreds of children to a life deprived of a permanent and legal family.

HISTORY OF A REVOLUTION

In the mid-1960s, Joyce and Peter Forsythe, concerned about reports of black children in institutions for whom no adoptive parents were available, made application to adopt a black child. Peter Forsythe is an attorney and his wife is a very capable young woman active in community affairs. They are white. Eleven agencies, four states, and twenty-two social workers later, their request to adopt a black child was granted. At that stage transracial adoption was unacceptable to most agencies. One social worker advised them to see a psychiatrist about their problem. The Forsythes have that advice in writing framed on their wall. The placement of a black child with the Forsythes was one of the significant steps in the adoption revolution. Behind this placement lay a growing number of problems within the child welfare field. Black children were virtually unplaceable for adoption. Black single mothers approaching adoption agencies were being told that the agency could not help them and, therefore, adoption was not possible as far as their child was concerned. At the same time there was a diminishing number of white babies available for adoption. Currently, adoptive parents hoping to receive a white infant wait about three years for placement, if in fact they can obtain a position on an agency waiting list. Further, there was a growing concern about so-called "hard to place" children—now more commonly known as "adoptable children". Such children were the retarded, disabled, and other boys and girls, even teenagers. Another factor on the adoption scene in the United States has been a concern for children in other countries, in particular Korea and South Vietnam.

Amongst adoptive parents an awareness of the needs of children has been growing, and at the grass roots level adoptive parents have formed themselves into organizations across the country—Open Door Societies, Councils on Adoptable Children (COAC), and so on. Such groups have placed pressure on government and private adoption agencies to rethink the needs of children who have the potential for adoption in that they had no viable family of their own. The agencies, or many of them, have responded to this pressure, or have responded to the new insight by taking action to make children available for adoption, and to find adoptive parents for the children previously considered unadoptable.

The Forsythe family mentioned before and the Council on Adoptable Children in Michigan were the prime movers in the founding of Spaulding for Children—an agency with the sole purpose of finding adoptive homes for children placed for adoption with other agencies, and for whom those agencies could find no families. Homes for Black Children in Detroit started as an agency associated with the Lutheran Children's Homes and is now an independent agency. As the name implies, the goal of the agency is to find adoptive families for the black children of Detroit for whom agencies formerly said there were no homes. Amongst the black families of Detroit, and using staff predominately black, Homes for Black Children has placed over three hundred children in 1970-1973. Under the leadership of Clayton Hage, Lutheran Social Service of Minnesota places over a thousand children a year for adoption including many who were previously considered unadoptable. Some of these children come from Korea where illegitimacy is a stigma that leads to rejection by society. The Holt Program is providing adoptive families in the United States for children from Korea, South Vietnam, and more recently Bangladesh. Other agencies have changed their practice and the hard to place child is no longer even the child who is limbless or mildly retarded, or with some other mild disability. Faced with the fact that there are an estimated 18,000 children in New York State who have no permanent legal family, recent legislation has provided for a compulsory review of each child placed in foster care or other form of substitute care every two years, with a view to assessing whether the child should be freed for adoption.

SOME UNDERLYING ASSUMPTIONS

Traditional adoption practice has been based on certain assumptions regarding the needs of adoptive parents and the role of the adoption agency. The main source of adoptive parents has been among those who are either unable to have children of their own or for other reasons wish to complete the family they would otherwise have had themselves. For most of these adoptive parents, and also for the community, adoption is the second best to having a family of their own. This is not meant to be an unkind judgment, but rather a realistic approach to adoption as an alternative to having children of their own. This group of traditional adopters, then, inevitably seek in the adopted child a biological expression of themselves. They hope that the child will "fit in with the family." They do not want the child to be different. They find it difficult to accept the child of another nationality. They have difficulty in accepting a child who has anything more than a superficial disability. Unconsciously, adoptive parents are seeking to have no break in their genealogical line.

This view of adoption is related to our view of parenthood. If we seek children as a biological expression of ourselves, if parenthood is primarily a matter of begetting and conceiving, gestation and giving birth, then we will want to relate any alternative ways of becoming a parent to this primary role. But there are really two aspects to being a parent. One is the biological aspect already mentioned. The other is nurture. We love and care for this child who is ours. It is possible for these two aspects of parenting to exist separately from each other. The biological process of becoming a parent is not necessarily related to the nuturing process. There are many parents who are parents in the physical sense, but who do then not proceed to the nurturing function. Likewise, there are parents who are not parents in the biological sense but in the nurturing. One of our problems in adoption is that we have tried, both from the agency point of view and from the adoptive parents' point of view, to provide not only the nurturing function as near as possible related to the biological one. Thus, often in the interests of the acceptance of the child, adoptive parents specify narrowly the sort of child they wish to adopt, and agencies bend over backwards to match child and adoptive family.

But what if we consciously separate the two functions? Is it possible either to help people free themselves from the need for a child to be a biological expression of themselves, or to find adoptive parents for whom this is not meaningful or necessary? Then parenthood as a nurturing process takes the predominant role. The child's needs become the main issue. Is it possible to base adoption practice on the love and nurture that we can give to a child, the satisfactions inherent in response to love and the giving out of love, rather than satisfactions based on the child as a reflection of ourselves.

In order to make a shift to the consideration of adoption as a nurturing parenting function, many workers in the adoption field are rejecting the judging role of the adoption social worker, which they see as almost unique in social work practice to the adoption field. This judging role, many feel, makes an adoption application a "test"—the reward for passing the test is a child, and the penalty for failing it is rejection. The traditional approach to work with adoptive parents is a diagnostic one, where the social work staff, with a "model" of the suitable adoptive parent in mind, assesses whether a couple measure up to the model within an acceptable degree, whether they should be approved as adoptive parents or not. The diagnostic approach to adoption has also the danger of being subject to the projection of the social worker's own expectations into the application process—our standards, our insecurities, our high or low expectations. "A social worker who believes a biological parent should keep the child born to her, will work with the mother in a different way than one who believes nurture is more important than reproduction. An adoption worker who regards adoption primarily for couples who cannot produce a child biologically will work differently with a fertile couple than will a social worker who sees adoption as a perfectly natural way to add to one's family. A social worker who is uncertain, or doesn't believe in interracial adoption will present the possibility of adopting a child of another race differently than will one who believes parenthood is not defined by race.

"The influence of the social worker's attitudes in other areas of social work is perhaps not so significant, as the client is not dependent on what the social worker feels, although the attitudes of the social worker must be considered. In adoption, however, the social worker's attitudes are significant, because the worker has control."[1]

WHAT CHANGES ARE NECESSARY IN ADOPTION PRACTICE

What changes, then, become necessary in adoption practice in order to meet the needs of children, and of adopting parents, and fit in with this new understanding of adoption practice?

1. PURPOSE

Clayton Hagen suggests that the purpose of social work is that a person be free to develop as a person with positive feelings about himself and others, and the world in which he lives and security of his own place in it. Social work's function is to seek to eliminate or reduce whatever prevents a person from achieving this goal, and to strengthen and encourage what helps it. On this basis, social work is appropriately concerned with programs directed towards enhancing the quality of life. In adoption, it means social work is concerned that an individual child had the opportunity for nurture and care and for positive relationships, and that other individuals have the creative satisfaction of providing for another person.

2. THE REALITIES OF OUR SITUATION

Some of these realities I have already mentioned. In particular is society's tendency to define parenting in terms of biological parenthood. Adoption has been seen as a possibility after one has failed to have "one's own." A couple considering adoption want a child like one that they could have had. This reality is reflected in agency practice which gives preferential treatment to infertile couples, and matches couple and child, thus reflecting cultural attitudes towards adoption and, to some extent, institutionalizing these feelings.

Another reality is the way adoptive couples feel about agencies. A book has been published advising adoptive applicants about the way to answer the questions put to them in adoption interviews by agencies. The book would be funny if it wasn't so true. Under our present practice agencies and applicants are often at cross purposes. The agency is concerned to talk with people about their motivation to adoption, about their own experiences in family life, but the applicants are often reluctant to discuss these matters lest they "fail the test."

Yet another reality is the attitude within our society to children who are different. Most of us feel some sense of rejection or withdrawal from children who are retarded or with other forms of disability. Our society consistently neglects to provide full opportunities of care and education as a charge on society to such children, and thus displays its ambivalence towards them. This ambivalence is reflected in adoption practice where we have usually said of the slightly retarded child, the disabled child, the child with a limited life expectancy, that one could not expect adoptive parents to accept such a child. We feel hesitant because of the unknown situation, in making much effort to find adoptive placements for these children. This hesitance in the face of unpredictability and the unknown also means that we do not seek adoption as an answer to the needs of the older child separated from his family with no hope of return. Older children remain within our institutions because we do not have foster care facilities, and we do not have the confidence to seek parents for them on a permanent basis.

But another reality is that these children exist. They exist without, at the moment, prospect of belonging to any family. They exist . . . . in foster care, and in our institutions . . . .

3. METHODS

Any method will be based on our purpose and the realities of our situation. On this basis many agencies have rejected the diagnostic approach to adoption applications. In its place they substitute an approach, conceptualized by Clayton Hagen as the educative approach. Under the diagnostic point of view, couples are evaluated and assessed as to their ability to be parents. It is the worker who makes the decision if they should be approved or not. Under the educative approach, the agency provides the information to couples so that they can make an appropriate decision for themselves. The educative approach means that social workers contribute to adoption by presenting a concept of parenthood which is different from cultural attitudes so that they are able to see themselves as parents. This concept would be a definition of parenthood as the nurturing and raising of a child, and a separate and distinct experience from biological reproduction. If couples are thus able to separate biological reproduction from parenthood and see parenthood as raising a child, they can see themselves as the real parents and convey this message to their child. This concept of parenting is crucial for adoption. Couples must have this information and an opportunity to rethink the meaning of parenthood if they are to help their child accept adoption. The educative approach does not mean that the agency simply provides information. Couples are confronted with the important issues in adoption. If adoption is based on a couple's values, they must know what their values are. The worker should respond openly to their ideas, and challenge the couple if he feels the couple are unrealistic or superficial. The educative approach is thus not easy. There can be more anxiety than under an approval concept. However, the anxiety should appropriately be on becoming parents not on being approved. The adoptive parent is seen as having a right to be an adoptive parent and the agency functions to help them make a decision which is right for them. The worker's role is on a peer basis, working with the couples towards placement, not on a worker-client basis, attempting to determine if they should get a child.

What we are saying then is that the traditional social work precept of the right of the client of self-determination is being given reality in the adoption field. As far as possible it is the adoptive applicant who decides whether or not they will proceed to adoption. There are some agencies who wish to take this to the point that no decision at all is made by the agency. This would concern one because it does not appear to provide full agency responsibility for the guardianship of the child, and the protection of the child against ill-treatment or other disadvantage in placement. Many agencies still retain the right to veto, however. In such cases, after the full educative process has taken place the agency will say to the parents: "I may be wrong, but I don't think you are yet ready for adoption." This does not mean that the process does not go on. It means that at this stage the agency feels that the couple has not yet developed to the point where adoption can take place, and they express a willingness to continue the process.

In actual method the group approach is often used. In Hagen's agency, for example, there are three basic study groups involved in the adoptive applicant's process. First, all persons interested in adoption are invited to attend a meeting to hear about the children who are available, and the questions and issues that should be considered in making a decision about adoption. The next meeting is more like a seminar where these issues can be discussed in depth. This second group includes persons who are themselves adopted, persons who have adopted, and persons who released children for adoption. This group is again one of information rather than implying that "we are here to teach you." There will also be an individual interview so that each couple can discuss their own personal situation. At this time couples can decide if they wish to wait for a white infant, for instance, or to proceed with an interest in children who are now available for adoption. If a couple wishes to wait for a white infant, in short supply as we have mentioned in the States, they are not given an application until the time is more realistic when it can be expected that a placement would be made with them, but the agency remains in contact with them to keep them informed about the current situation. If couples are interested in children who are presently available for adoption, the agency has further immediate contacts with them. These groups usually consist of six couples and two workers—one of whom would be the worker for a particular couple all the way through. The underlying approach to the adoptive parent is "we will undertake a study, with the assumption we want to place a child with you. There will be issues to be worked out—if we can't resolve them, we won't place a child with you. The security we offer you is not that we will give you a baby but we are committed to you." If they are not going to place a child with them then there must be honesty in the reason for not placing. They do not ask for references—you shouldn't have to get a reference to be a parent, but also you have to talk between yourselves.

They have tried to remove the arbitrariness of follow up after placement. They do have some post placement groups at which parents share how they feel. They have abandoned systematic follow-up to free up time to give to families with special needs, e.g., older children, handicapped children, etc. Parents know they can always come back. The agency depends on families telling them things aren't going so well. There is little home visiting. With all this they discover that more couples are calling them and are wanting to discuss problems than under the previous system. Also they find with this educative system of growth towards adoptive parenthood, their failure ratio is no more than it was under the previous system. However, unfortunately, there is little systematic built-in research going on under the new system.

The staff used to meet on placement decisions concerning which child would go to which family. Now they place children in the order in which adoptive parents apply to adopt. Parents can identify the sex, the race and the age. They talk with adoptive parents about other factors and also give them the option as to whether they feel that a particular child is right for them. A family take chances. There is hardly a child that they can't place, however, with a medical problem. They do not consider hair colouring and other features at all in the placement procedure. "Matching" is out, as it does not fit in with their concept of parenting and adoption. What they are basically doing is challenging people's assumptions. They believe in heredity but they are not going to predict the children's children!

4. WHAT ARE OUR PRIORITIES?

With these changes in adoption theory and practice, has come a sorting out of priorities. They know that it is comparatively easy to find adequate placement for the straightforward white infant. Therefore, priority must be given to finding families for the children who are not so straightforward. Consideration of priorities includes how the workers spend their time—in selection, placement, follow-up, and office work. The use of groups is not only considered to be an appropriate method in terms of theory, but also in terms of stewardship of time. They have had to consider methods that committed them to see more people with the same staff. Methods that released social work time, and ways of bringing together large numbers of children and large numbers of couples. Methods are not sacred. They have had to distinguish between what is desirable and what is important and what is essential. This has meant giving up practice which is desirble, when it prevents them from doing what is essential.

NOTES

1. Hagen, Clayton H., "The Contribution of Social Work to Adoption," unpublished paper, April, 1970.

SECTION II

CHANGING CONCEPTS: WHO IS THE ADOPTIVE CHILD? WHO IS THE ADOPTIVE FAMILY?

It has been estimated that there are currently 350,000 to 400,000 children in foster care in the United States. Of these, about 100,000 to 200,000 are said to be awaiting adoption. These children are already legally free to be placed or available when the right family has been located. About one-third to one-half of these children are nonwhite.[1] All of these numbers represent very rough estimates because neither public nor private agencies maintain statistics that would allow us to determine with any degree of certainty the number of children in need of permanent homes.

But, we do know that the majority of these awaiting children have special needs and are said to be "hard to place." What exactly does this mean? The North American Center on Adoption has categorized as hard-to-place, children who are: black children over the age of ten; white children thirteen years or older; emotionally disturbed and mentally retarded childred of all ages; children with physical handicaps; and sibling groups of three of more.[2]

The readings that follow focus both on hard to place children and on the types of families who ultimately adopt them. They also address the impact of agency attitudes, policies, and practices on the adoption process and final outcomes. One theme that runs through a number of the readings is particularly important. It forces us to recognize the influence of our own subjective perceptions on who ultimately gets placed with whom: the adoptable child to a very large extent is the child whom we have *defined* as adoptable. The same holds true of adoptive families.

Each of the articles in this section discusses efforts that have been made to broaden these definitions. It is obvious that a discussion of every type of hard to place child and every type of special problems likely to be encountered by their new adoptive family could not be addressed. Keep in mind that the kinds of children and families considered in this section and the problems they face are illustrative. They do not represent the entire range of experiences in the field.

The first papers in this section reflect the changing definition of the adoptive family, and the new ways agencies are beginning to tap previously unused family resources. Bytner et al., discuss the benefits of a range of creative, open-minded approaches to finding families, including using foster families as recruiters. Aldridge is particularly concerned with changing agency practices to reach black families for black children. Two articles discuss single parent adoption.

The remaining readings, with the exception of the last which is an illustrative case study, focus on hard to place children themselves and the kinds of families who have successfully adopted them. Two articles, those by Feigelman and Silverman, and Franklin and Massarik, are the result of research studies. The remainder are based on the authors' personal experience in child placement work.

Although the Franklin and Massarik article was published in 1969, the messages included are still timely and relevant today. The authors illustrate that the placement of children with special problems, in this case mental retardation and physical handicaps, has been accomplished in selected locations for well over a decade.

The fundamental issues are much the same now as they were then. Typically, children who are hard to place need an extra dose of love, encouragement, understanding, and patience from their parents. The majority do adjust in their adoptive placements, develop, and ultimately become a source of special rewards for their adoptive families.

The final selection by Heilman from a popular women's magazine, describes the experiences of one family who accepted two hard to place children with multiple handicaps, and also provides an example of one means of recruiting other families who may be interested in sharing their lives with such a child.

NOTES

1. Personal communication between Bonnie Carlson and the North American Center on Adoption, April 1978.
2. Ibid.

1

2

A POSITIVE APPROACH IN EVALUATING POTENTIAL ADOPTIVE FAMILIES AND CHILDREN

CHARLOTTE J. BYTNER, LUCY S. GRIFFIN, WESLEY W. JENKINS, AND ELEANOR O. RAY

The authors maintain that finding adoptive homes for children with special needs can be aided by a positive approach. They give examples of ways in which one agency reexamined policies and practices that screened out potential adoptive families or relegated children to impermanent situations.

It is now accepted that many children previously throught to be unadoptable can be successfully placed in adoptive homes. Agencies have made a strong effort to find homes for these children, and as fewer white infants are made available for adoption, more agencies are turning their efforts in this direction. Nevertheless, it has been difficult to make significant departures from long-established adoption practices, because of commitment to the welfare of each child. Pioneering in adoption requires more courage than in any other area of social service. There is such an irrevocable finality about adoption that a serious mistake in the name of experimentation is difficult to justify.

The conservatism of most adoption agencies should not be unequivocally condemned. It should not, however, keep an agency from attempting new approaches to increase significantly placements of children for whom it is difficult to find adoptive homes. This paper reports the effort of one agency to change its practices and approaches to facilitate placement of black, racially mixed and medically handicapped children. The primary change was essentially one of taking a positive approach in seeking out adoptive families, and in trying to find ways to bring together these families and the children needing placement.

There is nothing original in advocating a positive approach in evaluating adoption families. Many articles have discussed positive approaches. These include such concepts as "screening in" families (2:24 ff.) and the utilization of casework help for families with recognized problems, along with administrative innovations to change the agency's image. (1:292 ff.) What is different for us is the change in attitude on the part of the agency's casework staff. This change is one in which each staff member is committed to scrutinize every concept, policy or practice that might impede the placement of a child. Concomitantly there is the conviction that the vast majority of people who apply to an adoption agency have inherent strengths and probably at least average capacity for parenthood. Concerted effort has been made to discard individual value systems and to look at the prospective parents from the standpoint of what a child would derive from that particular family constellation. Whether or not we would want these same things for ourselves and our children should not be a consideration.

UNWED MOTHER AS ADOPTER

Three case histories illustrate this positive approach:

Miss Reed was an unwed mother who had kept her baby. When her son was two-and-a-half years old she applied to our agency for a second child. She indicated her willingness to consider a handicapped or racially mixed child.

The case worker characterized her as a very mature young woman who was open and sincere about her life situation. She had a great deal of warmth and sensitivity, even though she described a very unhappy and lonely childhood in the shadow of an older sister. Her mother and father had maintained a neurotic, symbiotic marriage with constant turmoil. At age twenty, Miss Reed had sought psychiatric help for colitis. She responded well and sought psychiatric help from the same physician six years later, primarily because of pressures from her family over her decision to keep her child, with whom she was then pregnant.

In the normal course of event, this bleak picture would have led to rejection. It was at this point that the change in attitude on the part of the casework staff became evident. The worker was impressed by Miss Reed's level of functioning. Her relationships with her son and his adjustment appeared to be well above average. Her willingness to accept a handicapped child, but preferably a biracial youngster, was partly due to an empathetic attitude about the needs of such a child.

The decision to proceed with an evaluation was buttressed by the report from Miss Reed's psychiatrist. He confirmed our impressions and said he thought that she had become an even more stable and mature person from the time he saw her in 1960 until his last contact in 1966. He believed that she had considerable coping ability and probably a capacity for parenthood well above average.

The final evaluation of this young woman described her as a warm and sensitive individual who had excellent parenting ability, demonstrated by the security and adjustment of her two-and-a-half-year-old son. That psychiatric help had been obtained at appropriate times was seen as a positive factor. She had made what appeared to be a wise decision in not marrying the baby's father. Wanting no deceit in her relationship with her son, she avoided any masquerade about her marital status. Although she did not flaunt this, her employer and friends knew she had never been married. She had completed college education and had chosen a unversity setting as the most accepting atmosphere in which to rear her child. She was financially prepared to give the children all the necessities and some of the luxuries of life. A close friend in her home city had agreed to provide for her children in the event of her death. Close friends and neighbors had been sounded out about a biracial child and were generally accepting of this. References confirmed her stability, maturity, and capacity for parenthood. That she was facing with her own son his out-of-wedlock birth was seen as a source of strength in helping a biracial child with problems of his identity. It was believed the two children would have a closer bond because of their origins than if one had been a natural child born in wedlock. Her request for a biracial child appeared to be based on genuine concern for the child's need for a stable family, rather than from crusading zeal.

A biracial infant boy was placed with Miss Reed. Indications are that he is being satisfactorily integrated into the family and the neighborhood.

FOSTER FAMILY AS RECRUITER

A second case involves the use of a foster family to find a youngster a home. This situation also required some rethinking and a departure from traditional agency attitudes about the methods of recruiting and evaluating adoptive families.

> Mike had been born with a cleft palate and a harelip. The harelip had been restored and surgical procedures to close the cleft were scheduled. Extensive orthodontia and speech therapy would also be involved at an unknown later date. Obviously, these handicaps made the adoptive placement of Mike extremely doubtful. Fortunately, he was blessed with a bubbly personality, with physical and social development well above the norms for his age. He had the ability to captivate people.
>
> The foster mother with whom he had been placed since birth was determined that Mike would have a permanent home. She began a recruiting campaign of her own. At first our staff was mildly concerned because the foster mother was demonstrating Mike's charm at every opportunity and making it known in all her contacts that he was available for adoption.

Such a departure takes the recruitment process out of the hands of professional staff. It completely obviates any idea of matching backgrounds (which most agencies deny doing anyway). It creates a rubber-stamp concept of approving parents on an *ex post facto* basis. This process goes counter to the belief of most agencies that they should not evaluate a family for a child the family has already seen and selected. Finally, the foster parents would know the whereabouts of the child if they knew the adopting family.

In discussing the foster mother's efforts to find a family for Mike, we had to come to grips with these ill-defined concepts and vestigial elements that remained in our adoption program. Our final analysis was that adoption placement for Mike was unlikely, to say the least. Nobody could sell Mike better than Mike himself and certainly nobody could recruit prospective adoption families with greater fervor than his foster mother, who was so deeply attached to him. We also believed she would be perceptive in "screening out" any prospective families of whom she did not approve. With some qualms, we decided not to interfere with the foster mother's recruiting efforts.

It was not too long before the foster parents sensed that a family in their church had more than a passing interest in Mike. This family had done an exemplary job with their own children, who were reaching adolescence. Just how it was arranged for Mike to visit in this family's home was never ascertained. Such a meeting did take place, at which time Mike had ample opportunity to worm his way securely into the heart of the prospective adoptive mother. The father, being more practical, was concerned about the cleft palate, speech therapy, orthodontia and the possibility of emotional difficulties. This necessitated another "arrangement" for Mike to spend the day with the prospective family when the foster parents had need for a babysitter. This coincided with a day when the prospective adoptive father would be home. By nightfall, he, too, had surrendered to Mike's engaging ways and Mike had found himself a home. The "study" was brief and geared almost exclusively to discussing the reality of bringing Mike into the family picture. A subsidy plan was developed with the family for orthodontia and speech therapy. Mike was subsequently placed and he is now well integrated into his new family.

BROADENING THE CHOICE

The final case illustrates the ability of families to broaden their possible choices of a child, and shows how an attitude about a child can help effect placement.

> Betsy was born with a kidney anomaly necessitating removal at birth. She was a fetching little girl, completely normal and healthy in every way. The loss of her kidney was not expected to have any effect on her ultimate development, health status or longevity. The child had never had any difficulty associated with the missing kidney and for all practical purposes it constituted no problem. However, it had been a factor in precluding placement early in her life. When the missing kidney was discussed with potential parents, she was bypassed for "normal" children.

The staff's concern for Betsy's future began to mount. It was recognized that the missing kidney had kept Betsy from being placed for adoption, since she was the only black baby girl the agency had not been able to place. At the same time, we knew this should not have precluded placement because it constituted no actual medical problem. Betsy's ultimate placement was made possible by an attitudinal change on the part of one worker. We are not even sure this was a totally conscious change in attitude, since only in retrospect have we realized what happened.

A couple applied to adopt a black girl as young as possible. The worker felt this family had much to offer. She oriented her discussion toward the possibility of an older girl. When they were responsive to this idea, she became more specific about Betsy and encouraged the family to meet her. This was accomplished by taking the child to the park and meeting the prospective family in a casual way.

In a discussion following this meeting the worker stated the family had been captivated by Betsy. When she was asked if the missing kidney had been discussed she indicated that it had been alluded to, but that was all. As placement became more imminent and still the problem had not been thoroughly handled, a question was raised about the possibility of rejection when the discussion did take place. As a matter of fact, the placement was effected without any discussion in depth about it. The family knew she had a missing kidney and that this constituted no medical problem. Realistically, there was nothing else to tell.

It was in a staff meeting later that we concluded the worker had handled this situation appropriately. One's initial reaction is that there might have been some element of concealment involved, but we do not believe this to be the case. Since the absence of a kidney did not constitute a medical problem, it should not have generated anxiety on the part of the staff. Focusing on the missing kidney would communicate the agency's anxiety about the child's acceptability to the potential family, who would follow through with counteranxiety of its own.

CONCLUSION

We believe a positive change in attitude is worthwhile for an agency to consider. For example, if a child had a functional heart murmur that is of no consequence, there is no reason to consider the child as one who is hard to place for adoption. If we can reduce our anxiety about the "problems that are not problems" and insist we have a right to minimize these in discussions with parents, it may facilitate placement.

If families can be recruited by foster parents for children with special needs, why be reluctant to have them do so? Most foster parents for preadoptive children have genuine concern for them and would never interfere after placement.

If families can see a specific child and then participate in an evaluation of the reality of bringing that child into their family, this may be fruitful. It is possible such an approach might be much more productive than one that involves a formless, faceless being who cannot be visualized by the prospective parents as a real living, functioning, child.

It is our convicton that such change in attitude on the part of an agency through its staff can be a distinct asset. It begins to penetrate the agency's philosophy and stimulates staff to find more creative ways to place youngsters with problems. It challenges long-held shibboleths as to what can and cannot be done in adoption practice. Most important of all, it can get into permanent adoptive homes children who might otherwise be denied them.

REFERENCES

Brown, Florence G., Jamieson, Ann M., and Dukette, Rita. "Reduction in Adoptive Applicants: Implications for Agencies—A Symposium." *Child Welfare*,XLIII, 6 (June 1964): 292 ff.

Edwards, Jane. "The Hard-to-Place Child." *Child Welfare,* XL,4 (April 1961): 24 ff.

3

PROBLEMS AND APPROACHES TO BLACK ADOPTIONS

DELORES P. ALDRIDGE

Some familiar phrases are "Blacks don't adopt" and "Black children are unadoptable." This work attempts to show that the real problem is not with black children or potential black adoptive parents but with agencies in the field of adoptions. Social agencies have to devise new and different approaches for becoming more responsive to the needs of black children. Policies and practices of agencies have to be refocused and staff need to be trained in the ethos of black people. The economic investment in new approaches is vital.

A major problem that black children face in being adopted is the label that they are hard to place. Adoption agencies in their failure to solve the problems of black children in need of permanent homes have projected the blame on the black community and the black children themselves. It is all too familiar to hear the phrases "Blacks don't adopt," "Black children are unadoptable," despite the fact that black people have a history of taking relatives, relatives' children, and neighbors' children into their homes (Herbert, 1973). While this has been a strength of the black family, social scientists and social practitioners have characterized black parents and the black community as lacking motivation and commitment to the concept of adoption (Deasy and Quinn, 1967). What agencies have in essence done has been to make black children the villians when in fact

Editors' Note: Copyright 1974 by the National Council on Family Relations. Reprinted with permission from Family Coordinator *23:4 (1974), pp. 407-410.*

they were victims of a cruel and insensitive welfare system. The label "hard to place" has contributed to an attitude of resignation and defeat in social welfare agencies faced with the task of finding homes for black children. Or, perhaps more indicting is the fact that labeling has served as a "cop out" for agencies that are reluctant to review their practices, and rethink their policies and standards.

Throughout the years adoption agencies have designed policies whereby homeownership, money, prestige, and education have been given far more weight in determining whether a family can adopt a child as opposed to a family's ability to nourish, love, and rear a child. The list can go on to encompass exhaustive studies which take longer than nine months (the time for natural birth), completion of endless forms, prohibitions against single parents adopting, and prohibitions against more than one child sleeping in a room (when in actuality this is a very common thing in the black community as well as in many other settings).

All too often it happens that prospective black parents are "screened out" rather than "screened in" in the adoption process as a result of these artificial and arbitrary requirements. While black children are still viewed as the villains, many agencies have yet to realize that many blacks simply refuse to go through what they perceive as irrelevant modes of operation.

TOWARD POSITIVE APPROACHES TO ADOPTIONS AMONG BLACKS

Efforts by agencies and community organizations across the country have demonstrated the reforms that are needed and could be used to solve the problems of black children without permanent homes. In recent years, numerous agencies throughout the nation have developed bold new programs for finding adoptive parents for black children who have been deemed "hard to place." "Homes for Black Children," a black adoption agency in Detroit placed over 100 black children in its first year of operation some four years ago (Fisher, 1971). In Chicago, the Afro-American Family and Community Service Agency received 115 inquiries about adoption and approximately sixty families subsequently adopted in 1972 (Herbert, 1973). The Black Adoption Committee of Los Angeles Community Action Committee was able to get 200 people to attend a single community meeting on adoption. From that session, fifty-five persons made applications to adopt and followed through on them (Herbert, 1973). From those efforts and others, there are four factors that stand out as being significant in getting black people to adopt. These factors can serve as guides for those agencies or groups involved in solving problems of black children without permanent homes. They are:

(1) Involvement with the black community;

(2) Philosophy and commitment of the agency or group;

(3) Aggressive recruitment practices;

(4) Development of policies and practices based on the lifestyles of the black community.

PHILOSOPHY AND COMMITMENT OF THE AGENCY

With respect to the philosophy and commitment, it is necessary for agencies to take the position that there are black norms for black children. The conception "hard to place" must be eliminated insofar as agencies and adoption groups are concerned. These agencies and groups have to begin to operate on the beliefs in and strengths of black people rather than their weaknesses. They need to know about the extended family network; they need to know that black people care and will and do adopt. There are some black people who are not committed to adoption and who will look at material things as opposed to adoption, but agencies can take on the responsibility of beginning to educate the black community concerning this situation.

INVOLVEMENT WITH THE BLACK COMMUNITY

Few agencies are located in black communities or have branch offices there. Most agencies are "downtown." An agency or its branch needs to be based where the people it hopes to serve have easy access to it. Accessibility makes it easier for potential clientele to know about services and those who are rendering them. Agency staff members, most of whom are white, throughout the nation have limited understanding of the social and cultural ethos of the black community. They therefore rely on the inadequate white criteria for selecting black adoptive parents. And it is becoming increasingly clear that agencies designed to serve whites do not serve blacks effectively (Herzog et al., 1971; Fisher, 1971). False judgments are often made about black families because they do not respond the same way to the agency adoption process as white families. Most of the difficulties as discussed here have been particularly descriptive of the private agency pattern, which never has been adapted to black children. While some of the difficulties have characterized public agencies, they have to be viewed from a somewhat different perspective partly because most black children are in the care of public agencies with limited staff of any color and limitated resources. However, irrespective of the agency's classification as public or private, there is the need for more effective staff.

An important factor, then, is action in the area of black staff development. Money must be allocated and competent black staff employed. If this is implemented and staff are granted the right and responsibility to design the processes, some meaningful progress will have been made. For years numerous communities have discussed the problem and developed solutions. So discussion is not the issue since it may simply be subterfuge for continued denial of homes to needy black children. What is the issue is money. Staff and money are necessary to place white children with white parents. Following this rationale, it is then equally assumable that the same is applicable for placing black children with black parents.

Perhaps equally important is the presence of black representatives on governing boards of agencies who are involved in the business of serving black people. Moreover, blacks find that policies are more responsive to blacks when blacks themselves serve on boards.

RECRUITMENT OF ADOPTIVE PARENTS

Historically, adoption agencies throughout this country have experienced great difficulty in recruiting a sufficient number of black adoptive parents for black children. Varied reasons—most of which are questionable—are given for the failure, but there are a few plausible reasons, two of which are the absence of knowledge about the adoption process and the extent of need for adoptive homes in the black community.[1] Factual information is sparse at best in terms of what is needed to adopt a child. If asked about adoption procedures, many black people give responses which reveal apprehension, fear, and unwarranted fantasies about the process.

Attention must be geared to:

(1) Recognition of the need for informing the black community about the needs for permanent homes for black children;

(2) Dispensation of information regarding the agency and its policies;

(3) Communication of precise information on step-by-step procedures for adoption to prospective adoptive parents.

Differing approaches to recruitment are necessary for reaching potential black adoptive parents than to white parents. Recruitment is largely affected by the feedback on the degree of satisfaction of previous clients. It is also of crucial importance to work with the news media including television, black newspapers, talk shows and soul radio stations to reach the potential black adoptive parents. Further, informal communication networks such as churches, community leaders and organizations must be tapped. Such resources and others ought not to be overlooked in the recruitment of adoptive parents.

DEVELOPMENT OF POLICIES AND PRACTICES RESPONSIVE TO THE LIFESTYLES OF THE BLACK COMMUNITY

A move to develop policies and practices based on the lifestyles of the black community is in order. In a number of studies, prevailing policies and practices have been criticized. Fanschel reported a high withdrawal rate among prospective adoptive parents and pointed up the area in which agency practices appeared to offend applicants for children. Even though a number of agencies have begun to look critically at policies and practice (Fanschel, 1957; Hawkins, 1960; Perry, 1958), there are still too many which have shown less readiness to do so.

The Office of Child Development, Department of Health, Education and Welfare and the George Washington University prepared a cooperative report (1970-1971) based on interviews with agency staff, black adoptive parents, representatives of community groups and organizations in five metropolitan areas. This report indicates that there are several deterrents to the adoption of black children. Among specific complaints about agency practice, top mention went to (1) "the time and red tape" involved in completing an adoption; (2) "psychological probing"; (3) "emphasis on 'external' such as housing and income rather than ability to love and rear children" (Herzog et al., 1971).

In order for policies and practices to be responsive to black lifestyles, agencies must take complaints into consideration and begin to act on them. Policies should be enlarged to include helping prospective parents in obtaining appropriate documents; setting more flexible appointment times; being more flexible as to where and how original intakes take place. More agencies have to move toward waiving artifical and arbitrary eligibility requirements in order to enable them to assess what is really important—the ability and capacity to give the love and security that will allow the child to grow into a healthy, mature adult.

CONCLUDING STATEMENT

Regardless of the literature which suggests that "Blacks don't adopt," and "Black children are unadoptable," the real issue is one of devising new ways and means of becoming more responsive to the needs of black children. And, until white run agencies can modify their policies and practices; reorient their staffs' attitudes toward blacks and the differences in their lifestyles; and provide equal amounts of monies and energies in the adoptive process of black children, there will continue to be a smaller percentage of black children placed with black families than white children placed with white families.

The successes of projects such as Homes for Black Children in Detroit are living testimonies of how when the approaches listed in the body of this paper are incorporated, the increase of placements with black families occur. Every effort must be made to help black families to become adoptive parents. They will come into and remain in an adoptive process designed for them. After all is not the whole point of the adoptive process to do whatever is necessary to "save the children."

NOTES

1. For counter positions see, Elizabeth Herzog and Rose Bernstein, Why So Few Negro Adoption? *Children*, 1965, *12*, 14-18; Leila Calhoun Deasy and Olive Westbrooke Quinn, The Urban Negro and Adoption of Children. *Child Welfare*, 1962, *41*, 400-407.

REFERENCES

Allen, Alexander J. A Commentary on A Study of Negro Adoptions. In David Fanschel (Ed.). *A Study in Negro Adoptions.* New York: Child Welfare League of America, 1957.

Deasy, Leila Calhoun and Olive Westbrooke Quinn. The Urban Negro and Adoption of Children. *Child Welfare,* 1962, *41,* 400-407.

Fanschel, David. *A Study in Negro Adoption.* New York: Child Welfare League of America, 1957.

Fisher, Clarence D. Homes for Black Children. *Child Welfare,* 1971, *1,* 108-111.

Hawkins, Mildred. Negro Adoption—Challenge Accepted. *Child Welfare,* 1960, *39,* 22-27.

Herbert, Alfred. The Problem and Strategies for the Adoption of the Minority Group Child. A paper presented at the NAACP Conference on the Black Child, Atlanta, Georgia, September 7, 1973.

Herzog, Elizabeth and Rose Berstein. Why So Few Negro Adoptions? *Children,* 1965, *12,* 14-18.

Herzog, Elizabeth, Sylvia Sudia, Jane Harwood and Carol Newcomb. *Families for Black Children: The Search for Adoptive Parents.* Washington, D.C.: U.S. Office of Health, Education and Welfare, Office of Child Development, Children's Bureau, 1971.

Perry, Martha. An Experiment in Recruitment of Negro Adoptive Parents. *Social Casework,* 1958, *39,* 292-297.

4

SINGLE PARENT ADOPTIONS: AN EXCERPT

WILLIAM FEIGELMAN AND ARNOLD R. SILVERMAN

A survey conducted by the authors compares questionnarie responses of a sample of single parent adopters with those of adoptive couples. The results obtained in this research offer support for the new and growing practice of single parent adoption.

Adoption by single individuals represents a relatively unprecedented phenomenon in the field of American social services. In the past such a policy would have been considered "unthinkable" by most agency workers. Earlier viewpoints assumed that only couples possessed the necessary role models and resources that could offer children psychologically supportive experiences. Today, however, child care professionals and social workers are increasingly aware of the large numberof children who are permanently estranged from their families. These professionals are intimately acquainted with the fates of children whose early lives consist of passage through a series of foster and institutional residences. Ultimately, these children are likely to be disproportionally overrepresented in reformatories, prisons, and mental institutions. Agency personnel have become increasingly receptive to new alternatives that could offer children permanency in a familial context.

Child care professionals have also become aware of the changing nature of American family life; increasing divorce, and the large numbers of children growing up in the absence of close association with both parents. As American family lifestyles have become varied and as single parenting has become relative commonplace experience, agency personnel have begun to consider placing children in one parent homes, especially in cases where institutionalization or long-term foster care would be the only other likely alternative.

Perhaps the earliest relatively large scale effort at single parent placements was undertaken by the Los Angeles Department of Adoptions, when forty children were placed in single parent homes during 1966 and 1967.[1] More recently, the Los Angeles Department of Adoptions reports that 379 children have been placed in single parent homes.[2] Across the country the number of single parent placements slowly and steadily continues to mount. Single parent adoptions have been made in a number of American cities, including Washington, D.C., Chicago, New York City, Portland, Oregon, Minneapolis, Indianapolis, and Bridgeport, Connecticut.[3] Nationwide, approximately between 1,000 and 2,000 single parent adoptions have been effected.

Alfred Kadushin's research has been particularly influential in stimulating single parent placements. Reviewing the research evidence of children reared in "fatherlesss" families in the areas of mental health, emotional adjustments, suicide, delinquency, and sexual identification he found no compelling evidence that single parent family life is inherently or necessarily pathogenic. He states:

> Research seems to indicate that children are able to surmount the lack of a father and some of the real shortcomings of a single parent home. . .the material suggests a greater appreciation of the varieity of different kinds of contexts in which children can be reared in without damage.[4]

Yet, the philosophy governing single parent adoptions has viewed these placements as less desirable and the single prospective adopter is perceived as an adoptive parent of last resort. In most situations, single parents have been assigned older, minority, and handicapped children—the least preferred kinds of children, whose emotional, physical, and social needs are considerable, often exceeding those of most other children. Although consistent with the laws of supply and demand and the child welfare perspective these placements appear paradoxical: those who are felt to possess the least resources to parent have been assigned the children who would seem to require the most demanding kinds of care.

Questions arise regarding the success of these adoptions. How well do children adjust in single parent homes? How well do their adjustments compare with children reared in two parent adoptive homes? Moreover, what are the common social characteristics among single parent adopters? How do these characteristics compare with those of other adoptive couples? In selecting prospective single adoptive parents, agencies generally insist that applicants have close relationships with their extended families to aid with the many demanding tasks of child rearing. How essential are extended family involvements for facilitating children's adjustment? Are there other sources of support which single parents utilize to meet the demands of child rearing?

A REVIEW OF THE RESEARCH

The limited research done to date indicates wholly positive results for the children adopted by single individuals. The earlier published study based upon eight adoptive placements, undertaken by the Los Angeles Department of Adoptions, came to the following conclusion:

> Our experience with single-parent adoptive placements has, to date, been very promising. In no instance have we observed regression on the part of any of these children. There has been steady progress in the development of the child as a person in his adoptive home, and in several instances, the development has been truly dramtic.[5]

A later study, also conducted under the auspices of the Los Angeles Department of Adoptions, was based on thirty-six single parent placements.[6] This study found that of thirty-six parent adopters, thirty-five were women. Blacks were overrepresented (almost 66 percent). Although the sample varied in its educational achievements, sample members tended to be more highly educated than most; half had completed at least some college. Most had close relationships with extended family members; 66 percent of the women were formerly married. Most sample members were employed and incomes ranges from $3,000 to $13,000. Although this research was primarily descriptive it was noted that, "these thirty-six case records strongly suggest that the children involved have found true 'familiness'."[7]

More recently, Joan Shireman and Penny Johnson[8] completed a study of thirty-one single parent adoptions of black infants in the Chicago area between 1970 and 1972. Eighteen of these families were reinterviewed three years later.

Like the Ethel Branham study most single parents were women; most were black; most had been married before. Although educational background, occupations, and incomes varied, comparable trends were noted with this sample: The Chicago group was somewhat high in occupational status, half of the sample were engaged in professional occupations, with low to moderate incomes; the median income was only $9,000. The group also appeared to be extended family oriented.

Although initial adjustments of the children tended to be somewhat negative, two months later, their adjustments were reported to be problem free by 81 percent of the parents. Trained interviewers substantially confirmed parental assessments. A followup study conducted three years later showed only two of the eighteen children in the reinterviewed families to have emotional adjustment problems.

Many questions, however, remained unanswered. Almost no information has been acquired on the smaller but growing number of male single adoptive parents.

Because these three studies have been completed with clients served by two agencies—the Los Angeles Department of Adoptions and the Chicago Child Care Society—it is unclear whether the social characteristics of these single parents accurately reflect the single parent population, whether they represent selection criteria of the agencies, local features, or some combination of all three factors. A survey drawing single parents from a diversity of sources and localities, would offer a better base to form a general picture of single adoptive parents.

Further, in discussing adjustments of adopted children in single parent homes, studies should be designed that offer some kind of control population, for example, comparisons with other children who were not placed in single parent homes. In the present survey the authors have attempted to address these matters.

METHOD AND SAMPLE

This study[9] was based upon a mailed questionnaire taken from a nationwide sample of adoptive parents. This work is part of a larger, now ongoing study of adoption. The data were collected between November 1974 and March 1976.

The sample was drawn from membership lists provided by adoptive parent organizations throughout the country. The single parent respondents had received their adopted children from a variety of sources domestically and abroad: private agencies, regional social service departments, and independent adoptions.

The sample of adoptive couples tended to overrepresent those who had adopted minority children. The typical adoptive couple in the sample consisted of white, native American parents who adopted a foreign-born child, most often from Asia. In selecting parent organizations to cooperate with the research, efforts were made to enlist the participation of parent groups whose memberships were acknowledged to include members who had completed transracial and transnational adoptions.

Attempts were also made to ensure the inclusion of at least several constituencies that represented in-country, in-race adopting families. Participating executive officers of the various organizations were asked to provide the names and addresses of any individuals they may have known who had adopted children but who did not belong to their organizations. Seven hundred thirteen questionnaires were returned in the samples of adoptive parents; a response rate of 60 percent.

A comparison of the characteristics of these respondents with those of other adoption studies, reveals that the subsamples of white native-born parents adopting domestically and abroad do not differ in any significant way from those respondents found in similar studies.[10]

SUMMARY

The data have documented some trends that are probably well-known to many single adoptive parents. Namely, that single parents are much more likely to encounter resistance from the various social agencies with whom they must deal in completing their adoptions; they are more likely to be turned away and discouraged in the adoptive process. Once they adopt, they are more likely to be subject to disapproval by their close friends than is true among other adopters. This uniformly discouraging response on the part of the community seems to be slightly more intense toward male single adoptive parents. Yet, these negative evaluations appear to be without foundation when one considers the outcomes of these adoptions. With few exceptions, both male and female single parents report substantially similar information on the variety and severity of problems encountered in raising their children as is reported by other adoptive couples. When controlling for the age of children adopted, both direct and indirect assessments of children's overall adjustments show fundamentally corresponding patterns among single parents and adoptive couples. These findings confirm earlier studies on the success of the overwhelming majority of single parent placements, and suggest that single parents as as viable a resource for adoptive placements as couples. In fact, given the present discrimination against single parents in the adoption process, the absence of spouse support and the more limited economic resources these positive findings suggest that single adoptive parents possess unusually high commitments to parenting.

Before being entirely confident that single parents offer similar benefits to waiting children as are found in two-parent homes, additional studies will be necessary. Future research should examine more objective indicators of adjustments such as school records, psychological adjustment test scores, and so forth, among comparable groups of children, in single parent and in two parent homes.

If future studies confirm the present results than there would be a need for reconceptualization of a great many theories of child development. Numerous viewpoints of child development maintain that two parent families are indispensible to successfully resolve the Oedipus complex, to offer role modeling opportunities, and to ensure the intergenerational transmission of cultural values and conforming behavior patterns. Most of the theories positing the inherent need for two parent family were conceived, however, during the early and mid-twentieth century, at a time when sex roles were far more differentiated and segregated than is true today.

Today, with married women participating in the labor force, and pursuing careers in formerly male-dominated occupations in ever increasing numbers, with household and child-rearing tasks increasingly becoming shared by both mean and women alike, with formal educational experiences of both sexes more nearly convertent there is considerable comingling of sex roles. No longer are men the exclusive tasks specialists and women the providers of nurturance they were in earlier times. With the increasing flexibility of contemporary sex roles, culturally appropriate role learning can be acquired from either parent as well as from both parents.

The findings outlined here also point to a need for reconsideration of the role of extended families in aiding and supporting the single adoptive parent. The mere availability of extended families, whether through living in the same community or frequent mutual visitations, has little to do with contributing to the success of single parent adoptions. A core of positively responding intimates, composed of kin or close friends—rather than availability of kin per se—would seem to offer a good prognosis for adoption success.

NOTES

1. Ethen Branham, One Parent Adoptions, *Children*, 17:103-107 (May-June 1970).
2. Personal communication, September 21, 1976.

3. Alfred Kadushin, Single Parent Adoptions: An Overview and Some Relevant Research, *Social Service Review*, 44:263-274 (September 1970).

4. Ibid., p. 271.

5. Velma Jordan and William Little, Early Comments on Single Parent Adoptive Homes, *Child Welfare*, 45:536-538 (November 1966).

6. Branham, One Parent Adoptions, pp. 103-107.

7. Ibid.

8. Joan Shireman and Penny Johnson, Single Persons as Adoptive Parents, *Social Service Review*, 50:103-116 (March 1976).

9. This research was supported by the Research Foundation of the State University of New York (Grans Nos. 082-7105A and 082-7106A) and the National Institute of Mental Health (Grant No. MH 27129-01).

10. Lawrence Falk, A Comparative Study of Transracial and Inrcial Adoptions, *Child Welfare*, 49:82-88 (February 1970); Lucille J. Grow and Deborah Shapiro, *Black Children: White Parents* (New York: Child Welfare League of America, 1974); Elizabeth Lawder et al. *A Follow up Study of Adoption: Postplacement Functioning of Adoptive Families* (New York: Child Welfare League of America, 1969); and Thomas Nutt and John Snyder, *Transracial Adoptions*, February 1973, Department of Urban and Regional Planning, Massachusetts Institute of Technology, Cambridge, Massachusetts.

5

SINGLE PARENTS AS "PLACEMENTS OF CHOICE"

KATHRYN DONLEY

Many agencies are slowly coming to believe that single parent placements are adequate for children with special needs. Still single parent families are often considered "second-best." In this brief and thought-provoking statement, Kathryn Donley, the Executive Director of New York Spaulding for Children, suggests that single parent families may be "placements of choice" for some waiting children.

In the last decade, many adoption agencies have begun to "consider" single persons as potential adopters. Most will only use single adopters for children who cannot be placed with two-parent families. (The translation: only for those children so handicapped by age, circumstances, or disabilities that most prospective families are not interested in them.) The reality is that in most agencies and courts, single parents are viewed as second-best alternatives to two-parent families.

Given that perspective, it is possible that for many children categorized as "hard-to-place," a single parent is the better alternative, the "placement of choice," because the particular problems of the child with a traumatic history and the special capabilities of the single parent? Some experienced placement workers believe so!

The *particular problems* of the child with traumatic history bear close examination. Many older children available for adoption are confused by

Editors' Note: Reprinted with permission of the author. Unpublished paper, September, 1977.

their history and unpredictable in their behavior. Familiar functional descriptions include: distractible, complex, scattered, having poor impulse control, untrusting, unable to use judgment. Though some of these children are successfully adopted by two-parent families, single parents demonstrate some advantages in placement. The *special capabilities* offered by single parents include:

— a high calibre of parenting potential (The screening process for single parents usually amounts to a rigorous testing of the applicant's interest and ingenuity. Only the most persistent survive the challenging course.)
— a simplified environment (Without a spouse or other primary family members the number of complex relationships is reduced to an absolute minimum. Demands are fewer in number and directions are less apt to be conflicting.
— focused nuturing (In the absence of other distractions, the single parent usually concentrates extraordinary effort on analyzing and responding to the problems inherent in the parent-child relationship.)

Other than "considering" single parents, we need to examine the possibility that they represent the better alternative for some children awaiting adoption. One-parent families are a growing part of the American scene. In 1976, more than 15 percent of the children in this nation were living within one-parent families. To ignore this segment of our society as a viable population of potential adopters, to dismiss the special capabilities they offer children, is to deny significant numbers of children the opportunity for secure family ties.

6

THE ADOPTION OF CHILDREN WITH MEDICAL CONDITIONS: PART III—DISCUSSIONS AND CONCLUSIONS

DAVID S. FRANKLIN AND FRED MASSARIK

This is the last of three papers reporting on a research project on agency methods and results in the placement for adoption of medically impaired children. The articles are a consensed version of a report by the Children's Home Society of California, at Los Angeles. This section concerns the implications of the findings for agency procedure and social worker practice in this area.

In the past, children with medical conditions were not usually considered adoptable. Adoption agencies, however, have slowly but effectively reversed a long-established trend toward placing the "perfect child" with advantaged parents. This has come about partly through a changed viewpoint enunciated by adoption leaders, who said medically impaired children were no less in need of permanent families than other adoptable children, could benefit in their own way, and should receive the constant, specialized, professional attention necessary to achieve this end. When, in response to promotional efforts, applicants began to consider such children for adoption, and to assume the risks of these parenting roles with conviction and enthusiasm, the change was accelerated. The purpose of the retrospective research study reported here was to examine the process and outcome of the wide variety of such placements completed through the Children's Home Society of California, in the period 1950 thourgh 1960. Part III discussses the major findings, reviews the factors contributing to the success of the placements, and states the conclusions.

DISCUSSION

The data showed that by the time of the followup interviews, minor medical conditions made scarcely any difference to the parents or the children. However, even the children with such minor conditions had been relinquished for adoption and placed at older ages than the children in the control group. Perhaps for the children with minor medical conditions the placement tempo may be described as unduly cautious.

Among the children with "moderate" or "severe" medical conditions, still larger proportions experienced delays in relinquishment and placement. Difficulty in assessing the significance of developmental deviation and possible neurological involvement, or in establishing a differential medical diagnosis, was undoubtedly a contributing factor. Meanwhile, however, many of these children were subjected to living in a series of temporary foster homes. In some instances, a change of the child's foster home was made after a period of hospitalization for illness or corrective treatment—a time when the need from comfort for a known mothering figure was particularly urgent. Systematic data from the preplacement experiences were not available, but fragmentary evidence suggests that the critically timed foster home changes may have been emotionally depriving and detrimental.

The importance of continuity in home and mother figure is clearly illustrated in one adoptive mother's report of her two-year-old son and his behavior when separation or pain was feared. This adoptive family was exceptionally warm and understanding in making restitution for the child's earlier chaotic relationships. He had been hosptialized twice for eye surgery before his placement at the age of twenty-one months. In that time he had been in six foster homes. The mother commented:

> Three months after we got him we kept a prearranged hospital appointment so the doctor could check progress on his eyes. By this time he was relaxed and seemed really part of our family in every way. But, as we came to the hospital entrance, he stiffened and screamed in his father's arms. We didn't know what had come over him. We did everything to comfort him, but he was inconsolable.

> Fortunately, a third hospitalization was not needed then, and we returned home.
>
> He walked soberly from the car into the house, then around each room, patting familiar things and furniture, saying over and over "home. . .home. . .home." For months afterward, he refused to wear a sweater or coat and was totally upset if he saw me wearing mine. Even today (age 10) he may get depressed and withdrawn if he doesn't find us when and where he expects to, if we're just a bit late.

Delay in permanent placement until a medical prognosis is established or corrective treatment is begun can inflict irreparable damage to mental health. The weeks and months used to determine the extent of a physical defect, or to await the optimum time to commence its treatment, may exact a far greater cost in imparied mental health than is offset by other expected gains. Our evidence indicated that the families whose experience with the children had been most difficult and unfulfilling, often found the psychological aftermath of a lengthy preplacement period and traumatic separation to be the cause of their deepest concern, rather than the physical defect itself. An important conclusion of the study is that such delays caused unnecessary secondary and tertiary problems; that agencies need to give concerted attention to placing these children in permanent homes as early as possible. Social wokers need to recognize that families have the capacity to welcome and cope with children with medical problems; that placement delays may be unnecessary and deleterious.

THE ADOPTABLE CHILD

Who is "the adoptable child"? Essentially it is the child whom parents can accept, who can give and receive love, who can benefit from family life. An ealier concept would have included favorable health and sound physical condition, but in our sample none of the defects, from minor to severe, excluded the child from the adoptable group. Greater risk and difficulty were experienced, particularly among the "severes," but even here few parents recalled disabling concern about the child's defect, or found the child's condition emotionally or financially burdensome, or regretted their decision to adopt. Much evidence pointed to a moving and satisfying experience for the families and the children. Confirmation of this broadened concept of the adoptable child is the second major conclusion of the study.

Particular attention was given in the analysis to the seventy-one children with moderate or severe residual conditions, to assess what satisfactions parents found in the adoptions and how well they coped with special needs.[1] As noted in Part II, a global rating of satisfaction and role fulfillment in adoption indicated that more than three-fourths of these families had developed strong, satisfying, resilient relationships; the adoptions were considered "excellent" or "good." Although it was important to communicate clearly to prospective parents what the child's condition might mean in the future, we also found parents in this group who had been able to cope well with unusual vicissitudes of development and with totally unexpected setbacks in the child's condition. One parent said of their child:

> Within two weeks after we got him we realized he was deaf, although we had been told only about his hydrocele and hernia. When he started walking, he had turned feet and stiffness of the hips, then later dental problems and allergies. But he's a beautiful boy. I coulnd't say I wouldn't want to do it over again.

Another parent said:

> He was later diagnosed as brain-damaged. I'd take him over again if I had the chance; we haven't had *that* many problems. Goodness knows, he's been rewarding!

For a third child, a new diagnosis of cerebral palsy, quadriplegia (considered severe by our classification), was made after her placement as a well baby at the age of four weeks. The agency was concerned about the parents' feeling for the baby and stretched out the postplacement period for many months. The parents said:

> We didn't really know why they did it. We were afraid they were going to take her away from us. We think they held up formal adoption for months to see if we knew what we were doing. We did!

Their social worker recorded that perhaps because these parents were very youthful and buoyant and had taken the child as a tiny infant so that she seemed truly "theirs," they showed particular resourcefulness in coping with the new circumstances. In instance after instance, there seemed no doubt that despite the medical problems, these children were fully accepted in their families, were cherished and, in large measure, were flourishing physically, showing minimal evidence of their earlier conditions.

A further conclusion affecting the concept of the "adoptable child" related to the parents' attitude toward risk-taking. Typcially, parents affirmed full responsibility for parenthood with all its inherent satisfactions and risks. The attitude was: All parents who give birth to a child take risks for the future; why shouldn't adoptive parents be expected to take similar risks? Workers may have underestimated clients' fundamental adaptive capacities, so clearly evident among the study families. Contrary to social worker's fears, the parents showed great strength and resourcefulness. The acceptance of risk, the struggle against odds on behalf of the child, seemed to call forth unexpected adaptability and yielded significant personal social rewards for the parents. Indeed, some remarked that as a result of coping with the child's problem they felt closer as a family, and had gained new understanding and insight.

PROFILES OF SUCCESSFUL FAMILIES

In selecting applicants who could cope with a child with a medical condition, the agency's professional staff agreed that they would search for parents who were generally relaxed about the parental role; who would concentrate on meeting a child's needs, not their own; and who would not hold too-high aspirations for him. They would tend also to look for rural, plain folk. A tendency to avoid the well-educated achievement-oriented urban upper-class family was implicit. Practice seemed concordant with these intentions, since lower-class families had more often been selected for adoption of the study children than of the control children. This over-simplified the situation, however. An analysis of the satisfaction and role fulfillment ratings of the seventy-one families with the most seriously impaired children revealed that the upper-class family was just as likely as the lower-class family to achieve satisfying parenthood with these youngsters. Failures were more likely to be found with the white-collar, middle-class family, perhaps too preoccupied with its own upward mobility to enlist fully its resources to cope with the problems of the medically impaired child.

The professional staff differed about the importance of previous parental experience as an attribute to be predictive of success in the adoptions studied. The data suggest that parents with other children understand the needs of the medically impaired child more fully than previously childless couples. Perhaps familiarity with patterns of normal child development aids parents to adapt more comfortably and to accept more readily the special needs and demands of the impaired child.

Two characteristic profiles of the successful study family emerged. In the first, both parents tended to be less well educated, some having dropped out of high school, others having had at most a year or two of college. The father was a blue-collar craftsman, skilled or semiskilled. Often technical training supplemented his minimal academic education. The families were not achievement-oriented, but were comfortable financially and eager to give their children every advantage. Some were not highly articulate; there was a sense of uncertainty as they talked about their motivation to accept the study child: "We just wanted a child." Social club and church activity played important parts in their lives. They strongly championed their adopted child and were angry when strangers, acquaintances, or even relatives asked blunt questions about the child's problem or his future.

The second profile revealed a different life style. These families were economically affluent, achievement-oriented, both parents highly educated, often having a college degree and post-graduate or professional training. They occupied upper-class social positions; the father often headed his own business or held a major professional, official, or corporate position. They were often articulate about their motivation for wanting the child: "We felt concerned"; "We wanted to do something special"; "Our children were growing up, so we could offer something"; "Because of our own training and understanding, we felt we could help this child." Professional activity was important in their lives, and for recreation these families talked of visiting their vacation home, sailing, or going camping.

Both types of families felt themselves to be close to the norm of the American family. Other children, biological or adoptive, often were present. Sometimes these children were older than the study child, sometimes close in age. Both types displayed a quality of parental attitude toward the children that was illuminating: They had an ability to see the child's worth, undiminished by his defect, they were undaunted by his developmental uniqueness; they took a hopeful, nurturant attitude toward his achievements; and they accepted his special patterns and tempo of learning.

CONCLUSIONS

Conclusions from the findings relate to the social agency's task in stimulating interest in adoption of children like those studied and the worker's role in serving them and their adoptive parents. The conclusions are as follows:

(1) Children with medical conditions of all degrees of severity and correctability can be successfully placed and reared in adoptive homes.

Social workers can have greater confidence in making such placements, knowing that in large measure the outcome can be successful. Even the most seriously impaired of these children can flourish, lead reasonably normal lives, and find and give satisfaction in their families.

(2) To interest the prospective adoptive applicants in children with medical conditions requires promotional efforts by the agency and the social worker's individual interpretation of the satisfaction to be gained.

Many adoptive applicants will consider only a "well baby." There is no question, however, that emotionally healthy couples can be found who will take an interest and can find great satisfaction in rearing a medically impaired child. Some with a wider tolerance of difference will not consider a medically different child unless the agency takes every opportunity to inform them about available children—at orientation meetings and individual conferences, through public relations channels or news media. For some children with minor problems, little special effort may be required. For others with major defects, great care must be exercised. General principles do not decide concrete cases, Justice Holmes noted; people do. Thus, an applicant couple should be given the opportunity to explore the range of difference that can be accepted, not in the abstract, but in relation to a specific child.

An example: In the last few years, the Public Relations Department of the Children's Home Society of California developed a successful format for conducting news conferences to inform the public via radio, newspaper, and TV about children, often with special needs, who are awaiting homes. At first considered heresy by professional adoption workers, these news conferences have helped produce a large number of "success stories."

Recently a five-month-old girl with an unrepaired cleft lip was described and shown. The hope was to stimulate an applicant for her from among the reading and viewing public.[2] In such an application, a minimum of three to four months would elapse before the family could be approved and the child placed with them. Despite the delay, a permanent family would be found for her. Unexpectedly, however, a family already known to the agency, approved and awaiting placement, saw the television program and telephoned. "Why didn't you tell us about her? We can take her," they said, thus expressing a wider acceptance of difference that the agency staff had recognized through its traditional family study process. Unintentionally, staff may limit the applicant family's horizon by directing attention in the abstract to a medical defect or handicap that the family might be able to accept. With the focus on a particular child, with its appealing potential as a human being, the medical condition may be clearly seen, but in perspective, with its relative importance better understood. Some of the traditional methods of probing applicant flexibility may be unreliable, and may conceal rather than disclose readiness to accept difference.

(3) Adoptive parents sometimes failed to grasp the significance of the diagnosis and prognosis for the child's medical condition, despite attempts to explain. Workers and pediatricians need to give careful attention to the most effective way of communicating technical judgments about a child's health and the medical outlook.

Participation by both the agency pediatrician and the social worker is helpful in discussing a child's medical history with the applicant couple. This team presentation can alleviate the parents' anxiety, particularly for those who are considering adoption of a child with a serious medical condition. The opportunity can be utilized to explain the child's potential, assess the parental reaction, and help reduce anxiety.

By taking this active role in the placement process, the pediatrician can reduce the chance that the prospective parents persist in misconceptions about the medical problem as its outlook. A further benefit may accrue. As a result of the initial consultation, parents may be further assured that the pediatrician is familiar with the child's medical history and should later consulatation prove advisable, they may have confidence in his understanding of the situation.

(4) Consideration should be given to developing further the agency's role and guidance to adoptive families after adoption is completed.

Once the decree of adoption has been granted, services are normally terminated by the specialized adoption agency, although parents are routinely told that they may contact the agency later for further information or other purposes. The study encountered some parents who wished to refresh their memory about the child's natural parents or early history; others who were uncertain about coping with the child's curiosity about his heritage and adoption. Still others felt uncertain in coping with specific problems at critical developmental ages in the child's life, and some needed concrete help in finding and using special educational, therapeutic, or recreational resources for their child. In the years when the study placements were arranged, 1950 through 1960, parents were encouraged to consider themselves independent from the agency once the adoption was final. A number expressed the wish to return for consultation with the social worker active during adoption process. Although these parents were usually referred elsewhere at that time, such continuing help now is increasingly regarded as essential.

Social work intervention could have prevented crises from developing within some of the families, particularly among the "severes." Help could have been provided through individual conferences or through specially organized parent education group meetings. Agencies should consider development of such resources and retraining of staff not experienced or comfortable in the use of social work methods other than traditional casework.

(5) Finally, variations from usual adoption procedures need to be considered for children with severe sensory or other residual defects, as for older children who have established ties with their foster parents.

If, in the agency's judgment, delays will occur in the permanent placement of a child with a severe medical defect, consideration should be given immediately to alternative plans for finding a permanent family. This is especially true for the child who established emotional ties with his boarding parents during a period of medical assessment or corrective treatment and with whom he is happy and secure. The advantages of guardianship, long-term foster care, or quasi-adoption should be assessed and balanced against the disadvantages of delay of unknown length in arranging the customary adoption plan. These alternatives to usual adoption procedures have the merit of uniting the child with parental figures early in the child's life, and avoiding critical breaks in establishment of his object relationships. In such planning, the understanding should be reached as early as possible that adoption by the foster or boarding parents would be desirable and possible in the future.

During the period covered by the study, foster parents were not generally encouraged to seek adoption of their foster children. Often this was not feasible, since the parents were in part financially dependent on the board payments. Nevertheless, our sampling included six such adoptions. Although no statistical significance is asserted, these adoptions appeared satisfying and successful despite the severity of the child's defect. For two of these children, adoptive planning began only after preliminary arrangements had been made excluding the foster families who had cared for them almost since birth. But the arrangements came to naught, as the foster parents could no longer bear the thought of having "their child" placed with "strangers" and thereupon voiced their wish to adopt. Indeed, with one child it was the healthy, enraged protest against replacement, accompanied by severe behavioral disturbance, that gave the warning of a potentially serious placement mistake. Only after being restored to his foster family after some months of separation did this five-year-old boy regain his happy disposition. Today, if foster parents have developed a warm, satisfying relationship of some duration with a foster child for whom a permanent home cannot readily be found, practice would encourage them to consider adoption and, if a subsidy were needed, would attempt to provide it.[3]

The prospect of future costly medical payments also tended to deter permanent placement for some children. If physically handicapped, a child could receive treatment under Crippled Children's Services until, but not after, his adoption unless the new parents were themselves financially eligible. Under a recent revision of procedure in California, a child eligible for care before adoption will no longer be denied care after adoption on the basis of the parent's income nor will the parents be required to contribute toward the cost of such medical care. Thus, one more deterrent to early placement of some of these medically impaired children has been removed. Adoption workers should support the passage of similar legislation in their own states.

NOTES

1. David S. Franklin, "Adoption of Children with Residual Medical Conditions," unpublished doctoral dissertation, University of Southern California, Los Angeles, 1967.
2. A number of interested applicants did telephone after viewing the TV show.
3. New York State provides subsidy payments for support of certain kinds of children adopted by their foster parents; California has begun a 2-year pilot project to provide a limited subsidy for children with special needs. Several other states have legislation concerning subsidy.

7

ADOPTION OF ADOLESCENTS

MARJORIE P. EDWARDS AND FLORENCE E. BOYD

The age at which children are considered "unadoptable" has been slowly rising. Many practitioners draw the line at teenagers. These authors maintain that teenagers, even those who resist the idea initially, may benefit from adoption.

As the result of subsidy adoption and biennial court reviews of each child's status in New York, more adolescents are being adopted—largely by foster parents—than in past years. Adoption plans for these older children have aroused negative or ambivalent feelings among some adolescents, reactions that many adoption workers did not anticipate. It had generally been assumed that these older children would welcome, as younger ones have, the knowledge that they would legally belong to the parents who had cared for them for many years and with whom they wanted to remain. That some adolescents have not wholeheartedly accepted adoption has been disconcerting and troubling to workers, to foster parents, and often to the children themselves.

As workers are faced with these troubling reactions, it is important to recognize that an initial uncertainty about or withdrawal from this plan for permanence does not mean that it must be abandoned. Rather, there must be casework counseling for the adolescent and the foster parents to determine whether the adoption plan should be pursued. In our experience the adolescent's uncertainty about or rejection of the adoption plan has been the result of either anger toward the foster parents because of a recent argument between the child and them and a desire to "get back" at them, or of the child's confusion about and reluctance to give up his identity completely by taking on a new name and a legal family.

The adolescent who in anger has rejected the adoption plan usually welcomes the caseworker's help in "straightening out" the situation and "getting him out of the spot" in which he has put himself by rejecting adoption, which he really wants. He himself has found it hard to tell foster parents he didn't "mean what he said," but with the worker's help he is able to do this.

The adolescent whose uncertainty about adoption stems from his confusion about or reluctance to give up his identity requires considerably more casework counseling over a longer period. He needs help in expressing his feelings about himself, his biological family, and his foster family, and in resolving these feelings to the point where he can make a decision with which he is comfortable about either being adopted or continuing as a foster child. In our experience two children, who after a period of counseling decided they wanted to be adopted, felt that they would partly preserve their identity by merely adding foster parents' surnames to their original surnames, thus keeping the latter as middle names—as many women do when they marry.

In all these situations not only the adolescents but the foster parents require counseling, often over a period, to understand the child's rejection of their desire to adopt him and thus legalize the existing child-parent relationship. This rejection is always a crushing, painful experience for foster parents, and one they find difficult to comprehend. Often several casework interviews are necessary for them to accept the fact that the emotions of all adolescents are complex and conflicting, and that in the case of the adolescent foster child the conflicting feelings are often intensified because of his life experience—separation from natural family, with the resulting insecurity and sense of rejection. When they come to realize that the child's uncertainty about adoption is rooted in these feelings rather than in rejection of them as parents, they generally express relief, understanding, and acceptance of their adolescent's initial reaction to the plan of adoption.

All our adolescents for whom adoption has been the plan have eventually indicated a strong desire to be adopted by their foster parents, and have seemed happy when the plan became a reality. We recognize that an occasional adolescent may finally decide not to accept adoption and to continue as a foster child, and we respect his right to make this decision after casework conseling has given him the opportunity to explore carefully his feelings about the alternative plans.

8

THE GIFT OF LOVE

JOAN RATTNER HEILMAN

This article differs from the ones that have preceded it. It is the story of Meg and Allen Tucker and their children Jenny and Brian. They demonstrate the way concepts of the adoptive family and the adoptable child are changing by example.

Jenny Tucker is a tiny, brown-haired, friendly nine-year-old who has plans to be an Olympic swimmer one day. Right now she reads "Nancy Drew" books, is at the top of her fourth grade class and tests even higher. Six years ago, when she was three, she was almost blind, could not speak or use her hands, was diagnosed as mentally retarded, had undergone five operations and spent thirty-five months in a series of eight foster homes, sometimes for only a couple of months at a time between hospital visits.

Her five-year-old younger brother, Brian, is a handsome, talkative little fellow, a blond husky boy almost as tall as his sister. He rides his bike whenever he can, practicing for the day that he can make it without training wheels. He goes to kindergarten, is learning his alphabet and, according to his father, is "full of the devil." Three years ago, when he was two, he was nobody's child, brain-damaged, spastic, unable to walk or talk, grossly overweight and considered retarded.

Today, Jenny and Brian are the legally adopted children of Allen and Maida (Meg) Tucker. They live in a pleasant suburban home in Virginia with a white dog and a spotted cat, go to public schoool and show no

Editors' Note: Reprinted from December 13, 1977 issue of Family Circle *Magazine(c) 1977 THE FAMILY CIRCLE, INC.*

visible signs of their uncertain starts in life. Except for their lingering physical handicaps, they are just like any other bright, well-loved pair of children in a close-knit family.

Jenny's eyes, which have been operated upon nine times, still need more work to straighten their alignment. (She has 20/40 vision with her glasses.) She was born with an atrophied undersized left hand, and her right hand is missing some fingers—both are due for more repair work. Brian's right arm tends to curl under if he is not watchful, and he wears a brace on his right leg. But Jenny and Brian are toally matter-of-fact about their problems.

Both Jenny and Brian were classified as "special needs" or "hard to place" children. Given up by their natural mothers at birth, they were shuffled into the foster-care system, with little hope that permanent homes would ever be found.

It has been estimated that there are as many as 100,000, and perhaps 350,000, children in foster homes or institutions in this country, and that the cost of keeping them there is about $1.2 billion a year. About 120,000 of these children are now eligible for adoption, and many more could be if ways were found to make it happen. Most of the eligible youngsters are "special needs"; they include children with handicaps—physical or mental or both; children who are "older," which means they are no longer babies (probably over 10); sibling groups (a group of seven siblings was recently adopted by a family in Pennsylvania); minority race children and those with mixed parentage.

The Tuckers went deeply into debt after they took Jenny, until they found a way to get help from local agencies. The child's operations ran up tremendous bills, despite the fact that their eye doctor donated his services for one of Jenny's operations and never charged for many office visits. Because of their problem in coming up with the necessary money, which forced them to consider the possibility of giving Jenny back before adoption proceedings were completed, they have put in many hours promoting the new federal adoption legislation. They testified at Senator Alan Cranston's committe hearings, subjected themselves to interview, gave up a measure of their privacy so more children could find homes. "There are so many families," Meg points out, "who would be happy to take those kids if they knew they could manage it."

Says Allen Tucker, "Kids with handicaps need a lot of love and a lot of care, especially in the beginning. But they also require a lot of financial help for medical expenses, special schooling, physical therapy and so on. The problem is to get it all together. States and institutions can provide the money, but they can't give the love. Families can give the love, but not too many of them can afford the expense.

"We feel that the least society can do is to help out. It costs much less to subsidize special expenses in a real home than it does to keep a child in foster care, so it doesn't make sense not to support what's best for the child. You don't have to be special people to adopt a child with problems."

When I visited Meg and Allen Tucker for a few days recently, I arrived at their small house in Arlington, Virginia, not knowing whether I would be greeted by self-righteous saints or perhaps flower-children graduates moving on to the next stage of an unconventional life. What I found was a warm, attractive, intelligent couple earnestly trying to explain why they chose to be parents of two handicapped children.

Although the idea of taking a homeless, luckless child may pass through people's minds now and then, there are not many of us who would consider it as a real possibility. There is trauma enough in waiting to see if your own children are healthy and whole; and, of course, it is certainly difficult enough to wend your way through life without consciously looking for trouble Meanwhile, we wonder, "Why did those people do it?" Admirable, certainly, but how could they take on a lifelong burden, a child who may always need special attention?

All right, why did they do it? Allen and Meg, who grew up in small towns outside of Worcester, Massachusetts, married in 1965 shortly after they had graduated from college. Today, at thirty-five, Allen, a tall, good-looking man who exudes an air of calm and reason, teaches computer science at Georgetown University in Washington, D.C., and heads its Academic Computation Center. Meg, thirty-four, a pretty, outgoing young woman with short, dark hair and a slim figure, is a former elementary school teacher who is articulate about where she is going, what she wants and why. She has not taught since Jenny came to them six years ago, but she is now going back to school part-time to get her master's degree in social work.

"We were the generation who grew up concerned about overpopulation," Meg explains. "You recall all those people who said they were going to adopt children in need of homes, instead of having their own? Well, we were part of that generation. We didn't really care whether we'd have our own children—although, I quess, we assumed we would one day."

Allen adds, "Both of us grew up with so many advantages, we felt we ought to use them to a greater degree than just plodding through life doing all the usual things. For some reason—perhaps it's our basic belief in God—we felt a need to make a commitment. Once we thought of adopting a handicapped child, it became our very own special mission. Now, of course, we've grown up a little and we don't see it that way anymore. Now we just feel like a family."

"We'd decided," Allen reports, "to look for a child who really needed us, one we could help. Finally, we decided to take either a mentally or a physically handicapped child, but not one with obvious traits of both because we didn't think we could handle it all. We didn't want to be hospital attendants; we wanted to be parents. We wanted a child whose future we felt we could improve. I'd been a counselor at a camp for handicapped kids, and Meg is a fantastic teacher. What can I say—we just felt we could do it."

By accident, Meg heard about the North American Center on Adoption and its special service called ARENA (Adoption Resources Exchange of North America), which acts as a clearinghouse to match up special needs children living in institutions or foster homes with families anywhere in the United States or Canada who want them. Through their local adoption agency, which did a home study and interviewed them closely, ARENA sent back information, including pictures and medical history, on a three-year-old girl in Chicago named Jenny who, the agency thought, would be appropriate for them.

The Tuckers went to Chicago to meet Jenny and see whether the three of them could make a family. "She was a little waif, sitting there on a bench in shoes too big and a dress that didn't fit, clutching a shabby, little doll, scared to death," Meg reports. "She looked retarded because her eyes were so crossed, she had eczema all over her face, and her mouth drooped on one side. Her hands, of course, were in bad shape."

"She appealed to us immediately," Allen recalls. "We really wanted to take her—but one of the things that clinched it was Meg played the piano and Jenny tried to sing along with her. It gave us hope because most severely retarded children can't carry a tune."

"To be totally honest, we decided to try it," Meg says. "We had a year before we could legally adopt her. We all got in the car, taking along her doll and a brown bag of ill-assorted clothes, and drove off to Washington. I'm sure as far as Jenny was concerned, this was just another frightening move."

Home in Washington, where they had just moved a week before and knew no one, Allen and Meg tried to settle in with Jenny. For several months, it did not work. Jenny would sit against a wall and bang her head, cry endlessly, drone continuously. She did not talk, could not concentrate, refused to become involved. She would not go near Allen or let him touch her. She was terrified of water and it took over a year before she was willing to get into a bathtub.

Before long, Jenny literally attached herself to Meg, whom she called "Jane" (perhaps it had been her last foster mother's name), refusing to get off her lap or let go of her arm. "And she'd keep on kissing me. Soon she'd go around and kiss any woman she saw. It was her way of trying to make sure she'd be accepted. One of our greatest triumphs came when she finally became discriminating about whom she kissed."

Jenny never misbehaved. "She was a perfect little robot," Allen says. "She was so scared that she'd do everything you wanted her to do."

Her first operation occurred not long after she came to live with them—surgery to remove scar tissue in her left arm from an earlier operation. She had had no feeling in her left hand, and the surgery restored nerve function. The next operation was another on her eyes, giving her a little more vision as her eyes became less crossed.

In three months, the Tuckers were in emotional and financial turmoil. Meg began having second thoughts. "I didn't think we were doing her any good—and I wondered if we were actually harming her. Allen felt left out, and I didn't want Jenny to sit on my lap anymore—I'd had it! It's almost impossible to say these things to the social workers at an adoption agency—but it takes a long time to love a child. It doesn't happen overnight. I'd reached the point where I hated the whole situation and I was filled with guilt."

It was not just the emotional problems, but also the financial load that was decimating them. Allen was making $12,000 a year, which could not possibly cover Jenny's medical bills. They were $6,000 in debt and sinking fast. The Tuckers did not qualify for aid from the Crippled Children's Bureau in their state because they made too much money—over $6,000 a year. Nor could they get welfare. "Everyone we talked to insinuated we were looking for free money," Allen says, "trying to make a few dollars out of Jenny. I spent all my time trying to find ways to earn more."

Finally, when they hit bottom, Meg, in desperation, called their Congressman, who listened and made a phone call, and a legal way was found to get medical aid from the Bureau.

Promptly, things began looking up. The special medical expenses were paid; Allen got a small raise, and they began feeling more secure. Not only that, but Jenny started to trust them. She began to talk, she did not cling as much; as her sight improved, her attention span increased, and she did a couple of "naughty" things for the first time since she had arrived.

"One day a neighbor and her little boy came to visit," Meg reports, "and the two kids disappeared into the cellar where we had some open cans of paint. Allen had made her a toy stove and sink, and we were painting them. Jenny knew she wasn't to touch the paint, but the two of them came up the stairs covered with it, tracking it across the floor, big grins on their faces.

"Allen and I stood there and rejoiced. At last, Jenny was secure enough to do something bad. What an accomplishment!"

"One day, Allen said he was going to the hardware store. Jenny went over to him, put her hand in his and announced, 'I'm going to the hardware store with Dad.' From then on, far from being shunned, Allen became her favorite person."

Since then, Jenny has had many operations on her eyes and her hands. She has good vision now with her glasses, and her hands are totally functional. There is nothing she can not do, her parents say—including crocheting, which she loves—except hang from the parallel bars in school and play the piano.

Jenny was about five and a half, and legally adopted for more than a year, when her parents decided to look for another "special needs" child. Through ARENA, they were told about Brian, a little boy of two who was "born dead" and had to be worked over for fifty minutes before responding. He promptly had severe epileptic seizures and was put on a schedule of eight doses a day of phenobarbitol. He was obviously brain-damaged, but no one knew how badly. He had poor control of his right side.

Brian stayed in the hospital for six months, then was placed in a foster home in a Southern city, where he remained till the Tuckers came to get him. "His foster mother genuinely loved him," Meg says, "so he was a much more secure child than Jenny."

"When we went to see Brian, we had to know whether he was a child we could help. You know, sometimes you can look at a child and think, 'We can make something out of this little boy,' and sometimes you think, 'No, it just wouldn't work.'"

The child they decided they could help weighed 42 pounds at the age of two, just a little more than he weighs now at five. He did not walk and did not talk, though he was a good screamer when he did not get his way. He was passive and unresponsive. His right hand curled up and his leg was obviously spastic.

"If he'd turned out to be badly brain-damaged and it appeared he'd never walk or talk, then we probably would have had to give him back," Allen says.

"Well," Meg adds, "he'd have had to be pretty bad. It's a very scary thing to know that you can give a child back. You have to wrestle with that, but we had to know if we could help him and if we could do it without breaking us."

For a long time, Brian was afraid to be alone, probably because he had always had the company of other babies in his foster home. For the first three months, Meg and Allen took turns sleeping on his floor. They kept moving closer and closer to the door and finally were sleeping in the hall before they made it back to their own room . . . .

The world picked up for Brian and his new family. With the help of the Crippled Children's Bureau, braces were made for his leg, and he started to walk. They discovered the Growth and Developmental School right there in their town, a school for brain-damaged children, and it was like the end of the rainbow. At no cost, a team of specialists took charge of Brian's therapy and in six months came up with the diagnosis that, as Allen puts it, he was "a good bet." His brain damage was localized to his right side, his mental ability was probably not affected, and he would be able to talk and to walk.

"With Brian, it wasn't a specific moment when we all began to feel like a family," Meg says. "It just took time. But this time I knew I wouldn't love him right away, and I knew when I was bone tired, there might be times when I'd be tempted to give him back but that it wouldn't be a permanent feeling. Now, he's totally ours. Jenny loved him instantly. The moment he came home, she taught him to talk and laugh, and she would let him hang onto her when he was learning to stand up. In fact, she pulled us all though."

Though Brian may never walk absolutely correctly and his hand may never be strong, he steadily improves. At first he attended the special school every day for intensive therapy; now he goes just once a week and does exercises at home. Both Brian and Jenny swim, ride their bikes, help clean house on Saturdays, and the whole family spends most good weekends camping in the mountains in their pop-up trailer.

"It makes us laugh," Allen Tucker says. "Both Jenny and Brian are good examples of how wrong a prognosis can be. If they had been treated as retarded they would probably have ended up that way."

"We were lucky," Meg says. "It's been like a miracle. Our only problem today seems to be other people, who keep treating Jenny and Brian as if they're different. We explain to the kids that the important thing is to do everything the best they can, to keep plugging, hang in there—and they do. They've got to love themselves the way they are, and that includes a lot of very normal and very special qualities in addition to their handicaps."

Jenny and Brian think it is a great thing to be adopted, and even brag about it. Adoption days are celebrated, just like birthdays, with cakes and presents. "They know they have genetic mothers who, for reasons we don't know, couldn't keep them," Meg says earnestly. "But the important thing is the love you have each other; it's who cares about you, who's going to be there when you need them. Our immortality doesn't come from our genes and our bodies, but, I hope, from what we teach Jenny and Brian—the values, the morals, the ways to think and to love and to be."

"Actually," Allen says, "we're doing this as much for ourselves as for them. When Jenny comes home with all A's when at two the doctor said she was mentally retarded, when Brian runs through the house and rides his bike when nobody thought he'd ever walk, our satisfaction is immeasurable."

"I watch Jenny laugh and make jokes and swim on the team and go off to stay overnight with friends," says Meg, "and I think this was the little girl who used to sit against the wall and sob and go bananas when she saw somebody in white or the suitcases were taken out of the closet. Can you imagine how that makes us feel?"

Section III

PRACTICE METHODS WITH SPECIAL NEEDS CHILDREN

Adoption II, the adoption of children with special needs, is more difficult, more time consuming and thus, more costly than the traditional adoption services offered to parents seeking the healthy infants in Adoption I. Good will and good intentions are essential. But the very difficult tasks involved in Adoption II need more than good will. These tasks include: recruiting and selecting parents; preparing parents, siblings, and the adopted child for the placement; and supporting the entire family in the consumation of this life-long commitment.

Competition among applicants for an Adoption I baby may cause great stress and anxiety for the prospective parents. Ability to negotiate through the application process may be the key to receiving an infant. The Adoption I worker needs and uses many sensitive skills and procedures in the evaluation and selection of parents and the placement of the infant.

These skills have been codified and developed over the years into a fairly distinct body of professional knowledge. They constitute, however, a different battery of skills than those used in Adoption II. In Adoption II, new approaches are needed in order to recruit adoptive families, build flexibility into policies and procedures, and provide services to families in crisis over an extended period of time.

Adoption II workers are rarely overwhelmed with applicants. Unlike Adoption I workers who often screen out applicants, Adoption II workers actively and vigorously screen in applicants. Indeed, Adoption II workers must interest adults in adoption, help them learn of their capacity to parent these different children, and inform them of opportunities to adopt from among a large number of different children. These tasks sometimes require missionary zeal if they are to result in placement of children. They require a new approach to a parent's assests and liabilities.

In addition, there must be a new flexibility in the procedures followed in each case that conforms to an assessment of mutual readiness among the child, the siblings, and the adults. The preparation of a child for adoption may be a time-consuming, difficult task. Preparation is essential. A child's past history of rejection, hospitalization, or abusive treatment may encumber his or her capacity to form the close attachments critical to successful functioning as a family member.

The Adoption II worker's role requires new definition. He or she must stand by as a crisis worker to give help quickly and knowledgeably at points of difficulty. This help must be available before the emerging bonds of a family become too strained or irreversibly broken. The family members need support as they develop mutual trust and commitment that must last a lifetime.

Adoption II workers must locate resources and advocate for their clients in the community. Clients should have access to a wide range of service including opporunities for temporary respites that can provide relief when the pressure is too great. Needs for such services should not be interpreted as indices of the failure of the family to meet adoptive parental standards.

The literature about the process of making adoptive placements for children with special needs still stresses a very intuitive approach. This reliance on intuition has allowed needed new practice methods to develop. However, workers in Adoption II must be able to conceptualize their practice if the quantity and quality of adoption services is to rise. If such conceptualization does not occur, successful techniques cannot be passed on to others or developed further to meet changing needs.

In this section, we have selected several articles in which Adoption II workers have attempted this conceptualization. Their successful approaches are thus more available to other workers. Goodridge addresses the use of the group for adoptive study, focusing on the importance of having a milieu and an approach that fosters honesty and communication among the agency, parents, and children. She considers this absolutely essential to successful adoption.

Bass deals with some of the agency policy changes necessary to prevent disruption in adoption, especially with older children. She emphasizes having older children party to the negotiations of the adoption process. Not to do so, she feels, duplicates the marriage matchmaker procedures.

Neilson talks about a variety of methods for workers to use as they prepare children for adoption, including the use of visual aids to help children make a better adjustment in an adoptive home. She stresses how essential she believes it is to help each child maintain a sense of personal continuity of present, future, and past experiences. This represents a break in the more traditional adoption reocedures. Workers have too often unrealistically acted as though the past could and should be erased when a child entered a new home, regardless of how old the child was.

The value of using crisis theory and family theory is conceptualizing problems related to adoption, and in developing a plan of action for working with each adoptive family is the subject of the Katz article. In the next article Bellucci talks about group treatment for latency age children who have been recently adopted. She describes establishing a support group for these children who have unique past life experiences that present life adjustment tasks. A group led by a competent, caring worker can facilitate the children's understanding of the impact of thier experiences and make the impact less traumatic in the future.

A sensitive case history of the preparation of a two-year-old boy for adoption is presented by Warfield. The child was so severely traumatized by his early experiences that he was unable to relate to new situations or adults. Warfield describes how she was able to help the boy gradually develop a relationship with her. This relationship was an interim step in treatment and served as a bridge to a relationship with the members of his new adoptive family.

We conclude this section with Churchill's discussion of what workers must do to assist a child and an adoptive family in the painful event of the break up or disruption of the adoptive placement.

9

SPECIAL TECHNIQUES IN THE GROUP ADOPTIVE STUDY FOR CHILDREN WITH SPECIAL NEEDS

CAROLYN GOODRIDGE

The adoptive study of couples interested in children with special needs should involve a special preparation difficult to achieve in the traditional interview method. One agency set up its own group study method that includes homework, movies, slides and tapes.

When the Maine Children's Home for Little Wanderers, a small private agency, expanded its adoption program to study couples for "hard-to-place" children, it was decided that the traditional interviewing method of adoptive study was not sufficient for preparation of such couples. Through attendance at conferences and contacts with adoptive parents' groups, the agency examined various methods of group adoptive study. Through trial and error, plus evaluation by the couples after each group session, the agency set up its own group study method.

When couples contact the agency about adoption, they are invited to an evening meeting at which the agency explains its policy and describes the children available. There is also a slide program, "Introduction to Adoption," developed by the Council on Adoptable Children group in Michigan. After a question-and-answer period, the couples are asked to

Editors' Note: Copyright 1975 by Child Welfare League of America. Reprinted with permission from Child Welfare *LIV:1 (1975), pp. 35-39.*

consider the information and contact the agency if they want to apply.

Couples interested in hard-to-place children—school-age children, children of minority race, or handicapped children—are selected for the group sessions on a first-come-first-served basis, with no more than five couples to a group. There is no matching of personalities or interests. The five couples are then invited for four two-hour evening sessions, with understanding that if one session is missed, the couple must withdraw to attend a future group, so that they hear a complete discussion.

THE FIRST MEETING

After all applications and reference letters are in, the five couples attend the first session. The couples and two workers are introduced on a first-name basis. No "professionalism" is lost, and discussion is facilitated by the informality. The couples receive a bibliography on adoption and child development. They also get a sheet of "unlocking" questions covering personality and marriage. These questions are strictly for their own use, not for group discussion.

A self-study form is completed by the couples in their spare time. The form covers information that used to be asked by the worker in several interviews, such as names and residence of parents and siblings of each spouse, how the relatives feel about adoption, how often visiting occurs between relatives, hobbies, and interests of each spouse, and a thumbnail sketch of each, emphasizing such questions as "Would you raise your children the way you were raised?" "Who influenced you most, and why?" "Has marriage changed you?" and "What experience have you had with children?" These autobiographies have proved useful as self-evaluation tools for the couples, as well as guides to the agency in deciding on placement.

The theme of the first meeting is "The Decision to Adopt." If infertility is the main reason for seeking adoption, this area is explored. Facts and fallacies about adoption and agencies are examined. The couples receive material on the effects of heredity and environment on the development of a child. There are also Public Affairs Pamphlets about adoption (Carson, 19171) and the film "Angel by the Hand," produced by the Bureau of Adoption, Los Angeles, which deals with generalized areas on adoption. The couples are asked to discuss only those matters about which they feel comfortable, and there has been no difficulty in starting discussions. (The men sometimes have difficulty in participating at first, but do not wish to stop once they start.)

At the end of the first session, the couples are given material about "telling the child about adoption" and about unwed mothers, to read at home in preparation for the coming sessions; a collection of "Dear Abby" letters is included.

THE CHILD'S BACKGROUND

The theme of the second meeting is "The Child's Natural Background." A film, "I'm, Seventeen, Pregnant, and Don't Know What to Do," produced by the Children's Home Society of California, is shown. The discussion flows easily into feelings toward the natural parents, how the couple can explore these feelings with the child in explaining adoption, and how a child may come into care of an agency. The discussion may reveal strong feelings about premarital sex, unwed mothers, welfare, neglect and abuse situations, and so on, areas important for the couples to explore. Some adoptive parents will be asked detailed questions by their adopted children about their natural background, and must be prepared to handle these. At the second meeting, the couples again get "homework" including "Only People Cry," by Alice Winter, about a young girl adjusting to a new foster home (Winter, 1963) "Adoptive Older Children." by Claudia Jewett, about adoptive parents' experiences (Jewett, m.d.); and an article representating a diary of a five-year-old girl being prepared for adoption (Bryant, 1973).

PREPARING FOR PLACEMENT

The theme of the third meeting is "Preparation of Placement." Discussion is based on the feelings of the child and family during preparation for placement.

ADJUSTMENT PROBLEMS

A second slide program produced by the Council on Adoptable Children in Michigan, "What Are We Waiting For?", is shown at the third meeting. It includes acounts by adoptive parents of placements of older children, sibling and handicapped children, and transracial placement. An attempt is made to prepare the couples for "the worst." Examples of adjust problems are given, as well as possible reactions.

Discussion includes postplacement reactions to such problems as bedwetting, overeating or undereating, nightmares, and honeymoon of good behavior and the testing period. Also covered are areas of general child delvelopment. Discussion usually continues into the next session. The couples are given articles on separation and feelings of grief when a child is moved from one home to another, and on the process of selecting a child for a particular family. A book, "Your Child From Birth Through Teens," by the Metropolitan Life Insurance Company, and a tape on family relationships, by Carl Rogers (m.d.) are also used for discussion.

FINANCIAL AND LEGAL ASPECTS

The fourth session considers "Financial and Legal Aspects of Adoption." Discussion covers the laws of release of children, as well as the laws of finalization, and the article "Statements on Wills and Insurance for Adoptive Parents," by the U.S. Department of Health, Education and Welfare (1972). Legal and financial responsibilities of the couple during the supervisory period prior to finalization are explained. Couples who have already adopted are invited to speak to the group about their experiences. At some final meetings a mental health film, "Who Cares About Jamie?", is shown, and a Massachusetts Adoption Resource Exchange Slide program about adoption and waiting children also is used.

During the last two years this method of adoptive home study has proved beneficial to the couples as well as to the agency. Its use has reduced rejections, since most couples about whom the agency has doubts withdraw from the group themselves. The couples tend to be more honest in discussions, since there are other couples who have similar feelings and offer support in asking questions. In the interview situation, couples are usually more fearful, and say what they think the worker wants to here. Sometimes it is difficult in the first group session to relax the couples enough to make honest comments, but once one couple express their feelings the others realize they will not be shunned by the worker, and do so also. At the last meeting the couples are asked to evaluate the group; they make some excellent suggestions. Most couples form close relationships to others and maintain this contact following the sessions. The couples have also requested postplacement groups for mutual support after placement.

PRIVATE INTERVIEW

After the four sessions, private interviews are used to decide the type of child the couple desires, and to complete registration forms for adoption exchanges. In most cases, the group sessions and private interviews permit deep knowledge of the couples through their interaction with others in the group, as well as their interaction at home. Even couples generally shy in groups find a common bond in their adoption efforts, and usually are able to join in the discussion. Most of the couples have banded together in an adoptive parents' organization as a branch of the Families for Adoptable Children.

AGENCY FOLLOWUP

The agency believes that one of the most important factors in the successful placements of children with special needs is complete honesty and communication. The group method paves the way to this honesty and communication, and to complete agency support and acceptance of feelings that the couples express before and after placement. After the adoptive study is completed, couples are invited to a once-a-month meeting for all who are waiting for placement. Audio-visual materials, such as the film "One of the Family," by the Los Angeles Bureau of Adoption, are shown. The continuous contact with the agency helps the couples develop patience and understanding during the anxious waiting period. After placement, frequent contacts are made with the family to provide support and encouragement.

REFERENCES

Bryant, Connie. (1973) "It's not Going to Be Long Now," Southeastern Star.

Carson, Ruth. (1971) "So You Want to Adopt a Child," Public Affairs Pamphlet No. 173A, New York, 1969; also, LeShan, Eda J. "You and Your Adopted Child," Public Affairs Pamphlet No. 274, New York.

Jewett, Claudia. (n.d.) Adopting Older Children, booklet produced for the Northeast Adoption Council of Adoptive Parents.

Rogers, Dr. Carl (n.d.) "Relationships With Our Children," Mental Health Info-Pak Cassette Series, Instructional Dynamics, Inc. Chicago.

United States Department of Health, Education and Welfare. (1972) "Statements Regarding Insurance Policies and Wills," Office of Child Development, Children's Bureau.

Winter, Alice. (1963) "Only People Cry," reproduced by the Department of Health, Education and Welfare, Welfare Administration, Children's Bureau, from Woman's Day Magazine, Fawcett Publications, (September).

10

MATCHMAKER—MATCHMAKER: OLDER-CHILD ADOPTION FAILURES

CELIA BASS

For success in adoptive placements of older children, agencies must try innovative approaches to the preparing of the child and the selection of the family. This author makes a series of recommendations about what such approaches might be.

The rising age of children available for adoption has made it imperative to look for innovative approaches to preparing the child for placement and to selecting suitable families. There is a developing body of knowledge, but the degree to which it is applied varies strikingly among agencies.

PREPARING THE CHILD

There is evidence of increasing skill of social workers in preparing the older child for adoption. Creative techniques are being developed with the recognition that the child's past plays a role in his present. Adoption workers are dealing directly with the child's anxieties, helping him to accept the facts of his past, the crises of his present, and the outlook for his future. A complete history is gathered and preserved whenever possible.

His behavior is interpreted, his special needs decribed, and his social history compiled. Medical records, school reports and psychologicals are gathered. Scrapbooks are prepared, stories are written, memories are encouraged. In short, the child is recognized as a total personality, with a right to participate.

SELECTING THE ADOPTIVE FAMILY

The selection of adoptive parents is also being refined and specialized. The adoption worker has available numerous guildlines in evaluating candidates for the older child. The early process is, of course, one of elimination. Motivation and ability to accept the child as part of his separate past are primary. The elimination system becomes more refined as a full range of characteristics is studied. These cover such areas as marital adjustment, health, finances, lifestyle, background and child-bearing practices. The worker then evaluates those ego-strengths considered essential for survival under the stress of adopting the older child or the handicapped child. Dr. Lorna Forbes, psychiatric consultant to the Los Angeles Department of Adoptions, has suggested eight adoptive-parent characteristics important to a successful adoptive placement. They are the ability to work with an agency, to express tenderness, to arbitrate, to be tolerant, to live nonisolated lives, to be resilient, to have a healthy ego that enables them to defer gratification, and a lifestyle reciprocal to that of the child to be placed (Forbes, n.d.). The ideal adoptive family is therefore one that is healthy, outgoing, tender, tolerant, flexible, resilient, cooperative and social. This is a heady combination, and one that implies considerable independence. Given the well-prepared child and this special family, the expectation of success should not be unrealistic.

ADOPTIONS THAT FAIL

The reality in present adoptions is a long way from what has been described. There are still too many children who are waiting and too many adoptions that fail. Some progress is being made in the first area. It is in the second that there should be deepening concern. Current valid statistics on the rate of failure in adoptions of older children are not readily available. Kadushin and Seidl (1971) did a study of adoption failures in Wisconsin between January 1960 and December 1967. They defined failure as "the removal of an adoptive child any time between placement and legal adoption." The study showed an overall failure rate of less than 3 percent, for children of all ages. However, in a breakdown by age they found that "age of placement is clearly related to placement failure, older children being overrepresented in the failure group at a statistically significant level." Their statistics show that for the placement of children under 2, the failure rate was less than 1 percent; those from 2 to 6, about 7 percent, and for those 6 and older, 9 percent. This was at a time when two-thirds of the children placed were under 2 years old.

Statistics for public welfare agencies in California show an increasing percentage of children returned from adoptive homes in relation to the number placed. In 1970 it was 2.7 percent; in 1971 it was 2.8 percent; in 1972 it was 5.7 percent and in 1973 it was 7.6 percent. These statistics are not broken down by age, but it is reasonable to assume that they reflect the increasing number of older children being placed (Public Welfare in California 1972-1972).

CALIFORNIA SURVEY

An unpublished survey of failed adoptions in the Bay Area counties of California by Bass and Mazur showed age to be the single most significant factor. The cases of 53 children returned from adoption in the 2-year period from 1972-1974 were reviewed. The older the child at the time of placement, the greater the hazards in that placement. Forty-two of the children (79 percent) were over the age of 2, and of these 19 (35 percent of the total) were in the 9-to-12 year age range. The most frequently stated reasons for the failures were behavior problems of the children; disruption of the family functioning; inability of the child to meet family's expectations; and internal marital or family problems (Bass and Mazur, n.d.)

The primary aim in adoptions should be to reverse the trend of increasing failures while continuing to place the older children. A placement failure may yield a maladaptive adult. Bringing such failures to an irreducible minimum requires agencies to modify old structures and to individualize each situation. The specializations of work with the child and selection of the families have made significant strides, but not congruent ones. It is in the coordination of the two areas of expertise that the greatest weakness is found. The decision-making process that brings family and child together often remains archaic. It resembles the traditional marriage-matchmaker concentp. The potential partners in a lifetime commitment are expected to remain on the periphery, without any communication, until the decision makers and negotiators have made a selection. The typical process involves a committee of adoption workers evaluating children and homes, mostly from written material. The technique might start out with the simplest descriptive facts, e.g., a 7-year-old boy needs a home and families willing to consider such a child are available. The process may move on to various degrees of matching until a single selection is made.

SUGGESTED CHANGES

Adoption of an older child is like a marriage. As Bell (1959) says, "It is a process whereby individuals, already equipped with consciousness, memories, patterns of thought and reaction, and large stores of life experience, link their lives together." Given this as a reasonable assessment, would it not appear appropriate to allow more self-determination among the primary parties involved? Unique families are approved for their strengths and then are expected to accept in a dependent manner the decisions made for them. Typically, a single child is presented to a family by means of an oral description and an appealing picture, and a tentative commitment is expected.

> Mr. and Mrs. C were a young black couple from a working-class background who had achieved at a much higher level than any previous member of their families. They were bright, ambitious and aware. They had a natural daughter and wished to add to their family a son in the 4-year age range. They were accustomed to making decisions for themselves. They were not receptive to agencies or bureaucratic procedures. Mr. C, who had early unpleasant memories of social workers, made his feelings clearly known in the first interview. As the home study proceeded, his good humor prevailed and he participated in good spirit. After the approval, the worker researched available children, of whom there were many, and a selection was made. She was stunned to meet with active resistance to the agency choice. Mr. and Mrs. C made it clear that they did not think it reasonable for a middle-aged white woman to decide what might be right for them, and the worker accepted their objections as valid. It was agreed that several children would be described in detail and that the final choice would be theirs. A successful placement was made.

LACK OF TRUST

Another example of the wide gap between agency and family is the lack of trust sometimes revealed in the sharing of significant information. Occasionally sensitive information is withheld on the assumption that the adopting family might react negatively. Value judgments of workers are placed on what is good and what is bad. This technique is morally questionable. If the life and future of a child are to be entrusted to his new parents, they can be trusted with all the information pertinent to his individuality.

> Mr. and Mrs. A, a couple in their 30's, were experienced parents. They were mature, responsible persons accustomed to cooperating with their children's schools. They had two normal, healthy youngsters. They came to the agency secure in the knowledge of their own competency and were eager to share their good fortune with another child. They were expectant that any child placed in their home was likely to have a difficult adjustment period and some educational deficiencies. A child with a deprived early history and a chaotic foster home placement was presented to them. They showed considerable interest, but requested more detailed information. The agency had extensive material available on family history, psychological, school evaluations, etc. This material revealed a mildly disturbed child with learning disabilities. The agency refused to give the full details to the family, but only summarized them on the grounds that the information was for professional use only. Mr. and Mrs. A expressed considerable concern about what was left out, and their fantasies assumed even more serious problems than the reality. They therefore elected not to proceed with this child.

Dr. Forbes, in her discussion of selection of families, refers to "high-risk" families, those who have only a limited number of desired characteristics. She does not recommend ruling out such parents, but speaks instead of successful placements that may result from "balancing the degree of the woundedness" between parents and child (Forbes, n.d.).

> Joey was diagnosed as having severe neurological handicaps. He had spent the first 8 years of life in a succession of foster homes in placements that ended for various reasons, not all of which were outright rejections of Joey. Joey's interpretation was, nevertheless, one of being unloved and therefore unlovable. The family with which Joey was finally placed was completely unorthodox in every respect, and in the not-so-distant past would have been rejected summarily. It was a second marriage for the mother, who was significantly older than the father; and she was older than one would normally consider for an 8-year-old child; they had already reared a large family of children from the mother's first marriage; they had haphazard income and unconventional life style, and their home frequently filled with returned children and grandchildren, seemed chaotic. But they took Joey, nurtured and healed him and loved him for what he was. It has been 2 years since he was placed and he is developing a sense of self-esteem and personal value as a child who is wanted.

DISCUSSION

Goldstein, Freud, and Solnit (1973) emphasize the significance of time in the child's concept of continuity. Speed relative to the child's needs is therefore essential in selecting a home for the child. They propose that the "child's placement be treated . . . as a matter of urgency" and that the final decision be accelerated. We cannot afford the luxury of lengthy deliberations. It is essential that agencies have approved families readily available so that a placement need not be delayed for lack of suitable choices. To expedite this, agencies must use creative, innovative approaches. The following are some suggestions:

(1) Reduce objective standards about age, size of family, life style, etc., to an absolute minimum. The traditional ideal family does not necessaily meet the needs of a particular child.

(2) Discard concepts like primogeniture, middle-child status, large families as undesirable, or the need for an adoptive child to be the youngest. If the parents have the capacity to individualize, the child can fit anywhere in the family constellation.

(3) Involve the families in all the procedures of the home study, including the selection process and the decision making, to as great a degree as possible.

(4) Respect the right of the child to have full knowledge as to what is happening to him, and to make determinations for himself where feasible.

(5) Establish mutual trust and respect. Prospective parents should have all information on the child's history, without judgment as to what is good or bad. The child has the right to this same knowledge, without sugar-coating.

(6) Provide supportive services after the adoption as needed. This may mean financial aid, psychiatric help, psychological testing and counseling upon request, without a means test.

(7) Do not allow the role of the worker to be intrusive. Life styles are peculiar to each individual family, childrearing standards can vary, educational expectations differ, and the worker's lifestyle, standards and expectations are not the ideal against which others are to be judged. The worker must be available to provide strength, support, guidance and empathy when it is asked for, but she must also be able to maintain some distnce if the family is capable of going it alone.

(8) Be flexible about the supervisory period during which the agency remains involved. For some families a minimum time to meet legal requirements is all that is necessary. For others, agency services

may extend over a longer period. The legalization of an adoption should not signal an abrupt end to service. The door should always be open for counseling, group participation or referral to other community resources.

CONCLUSION

The primary function of adoption agencies today is to place in the most suitable home and in the shortest possible time that group of children known as "hard to place." These children become readily placeable if agencies and workers exercise ingenuity and imagination, and can disassociate from red tape and the ways they used to know. All parties to the adoption, i.e., agency, child, adoptive parents and siblings, must be full working paries in an undertaking fraught with hazards. Full involvement by the participants can overcome these hazards.

REFERENCES

Bass, Celia, and Mazur, Vivian. Unpublished survey of children returned from adoptive placement in Bay Area Counties of Northern California.

Bell, Velma. (1959) "Special Considerations in the Adoption of the Older Child," *Social Casework,* XL (June).

Forbes, Lorna. (n.d.) Remarks at a workshop on adopting older children.

Goldstein, Joseph; Freud, Anna, and Solnit, Albert J. (1973) *Beyond the Best Interests of the Child.* New York: Free Press.

Kadushin, Alfred, and Seidl, Frederick W. (1971) "Adoption Failure: A Social Work Postmorten," Social Work, XVI (July).

Public Welfare in California 1972-1973, Series AR 1-15. State of California Health and Welfare Agency, Department of Social Welfare.

11

PLACING OLDER CHILDREN IN ADOPTIVE HOMES: AN EXCERPT

JACQUELINE NEILSON

The relationship between the older child and the worker is a foundation for successful placement of older children. This article discusses a broad range of activities and techniques for workers to use with the child, the foster family, and adoptive applicants in the process of placing an older child.

In every child welfare program there are older children who could be adopted—if sufficient attention to their needs were given and the right family found for them. These children are the "orphans of the living," abandoned, neglected and/or abused children—who are relegated to foster care. All of these older children have the same right to a permanent adoptive family as the abandoned, orphaned or relinquished infant.

Based on our experience, we have developed a philosophy, policy, and method that are applied to a program that is not necessarily new but is carefully coordinated to increase appreciably the chances that children over six will find a permanent family.

Because we believe that a child who needs a family *is* adoptable, we have never has an upper age limit for placing a child for adoption. We believe that failures in adoptive placements of older children are more likely to occur if the agency social worker does not fully understand the

Editors' Note: Reprinted from Children Today, *November-December 1972, pp. 7-13.*

child and the potential of adoptive families. The foundation of our program is the relationship between the child and the worker who is going to make the placement. All other aspects are secondary. Our social workers are chosen on the basis of their interest and innate skills in handling children, as well as for their professional backgrounds. They are trained to acquire a thorough knowledge of the personalities of the individual children and to become familiar with all aspects of their behavior. Because our workers are required to visit a child at least once a week, we have found that ten to twelve active cases is a reasonable maximum for each worker in the Older Children's Unit.

Many of our children, although often originally referred by the Court or a child protection agency, are relinquished directly to us by their natural parents. This gives us a unique opportunity to understand the child's background. However, the worker's job is two-pronged since he or she must help the child to understand and distressing situation, and at the same time help his or her parents to explore their feelings and form the best plan for their child.

During this period, however, we do not consider the case as simply an adoption one. We view it more as a problem of planning for the child's future, with adoption held out as one posibility. Our workers are prepared to explore and implement any appropriate plan that the parents consider best for their child's care, even if adoption is rejected.

WORKING WITH THE CHILD

The social worker must earn the trust of the child, who needs time to understand how much he can trust himself with the worker. Too often we go to a child and try to explain a series of events in a brief period. A better approach is to present the child with a realistic picture of his circumstances from the very beginning. For example, when first placing a child in a foster home, the worker might say, "This is a foster home where you will stay right now, but we will be looking for a permanent home for you." At the time the child is freed by court action, the worker might say: "Your own mother had some grown-up problems of her own. She felt scared and ran away. The judge feels you need new parents who will take care of you."

What gives a child confidence in his social worker is having the opportunity, over a long period of time, to express his feelings about what is happening to him. If the child comes to realize that the worker truly does know how he feels, he will be more willing to trust the worker when she finally says: "I think I have found the right family for you; I can't be sure until you get to meet each other." From the first contact, the worker anticipates that the child will some day have to accept a permanent home with a totally strange family on the strength of his faith in the worker's genuine concern for his future.

How a child approaches his situation, what his feelings are, and what he is willing to give of himself in the experience are directly related to the quality of his relationship with the person making the decision on his behalf. Our workers recognize from the very first day that they must help children face reality.

When a parent has treated a child brutally or neglectfully, the fact also must be faced and discussed. The worker must not be judgemental, because, in a sense, this child is a part of the neglectful parent and may come to fear the worker's judgemental attitude. A child cannot separate himself from his own parent situation—either the real one or the fantasy one that he may have built up in his mind over the years, unless he has some other reality to take its place. In many respects, the problem of a parent's relinquishing a child is only half the task. There is also the need to help the child understand his parent enough to accept the meaning of the latter's action so that he, in turn may relinquish the parent. Some children can do this totally, some only partially, and some never can do this. The quality of a child's relationship with a new family will relate very much to his capability in this respect.

HANDLING SEPARATION

The worker must understand and help the child face the tremendous impact separation and grief have upon him, a very difficult circumstance. While the child must receive the comfort of human companionship and understanding during this period, he must not be "comforted out of the feeling of grief." The worker's willingness to permit the child honest mourning and to talk about these feelings will help the child develop a sense of reality about what is actually going on. Otherwise the child may blame himself for the unhappy experience.

The truth of some children's experiences is very harsh. If they are unable to accept it, they will adopt any of a number of defenses commonly used to avoid feeling which cannot be tolerated at the moment. The worker must hold the truth available and be sensitive enough to know when the child has become ready to cope with it.

The worker must also have the capacity to withstand the emotional barrage that a child can direct toward him in times of distress. A child may need the worker to mother him, and the worker has to be able to do this, still realizing that her role is that of a worker and not a mother. She must help the child to understand what is going on, so that the child himself does not become confused in roles. The worker needs the kind of equilibrium and flexibility that will permit the mothering of a child without either of them being confused as to who the mother will be in reality . . . .

THE AGENCY AND THE FOSTER PARENTS

A child cannot survive simply by being understood; he also has to be cared for, and these two factors must be closely coordinated to give a child the feeling that there is a group of people who are concerned about his welfare. The social worker must help the child digest his foster home experience. It is also the social worker who helps the foster family to understand where it fits into the agency program. As the foster family is made aware of the importance of their contribution to the study of the child, they and the worker can form an effective team to help the child alter behavior that may be unattractive to himself and to others . . . .

Our Adoption Selection also conducts several discussion groups where families get together under the guidance of the foster family coordinator, to discuss the problems of raising children who are being prepared for adoption. Other work with foster parents includes film showings, lectures by community professionals, and a recommended reading program.

Agency staff who work with applicant families and older children also meet in a series of seminars so that each may be familiar with the intricacies of the others' assignments and coordinate them more effectively. Applicant workers see the children often, both formally and informally, in person and through pictures, slides and movies, so that they will have intimate knowledge about the children who are available and be better able to recognize appropriate families for them.

INTERVIEWING A CHILD

In our culture, adults tend to distrust communication that is not verbal. A child, however, does not always have the words to describe his feelings accurately, even if he recognizes what they are. In communicating with the child, the worker soon finds that much of the time he has to rely on nonverbal communication. For example, a child who is saying that he does not care that his mother has left him because this new place has plenty of toys and a dog and a kitty might betray his true feelings by the expression on his face or the tension in his body.

If there is no evidence of tension, perhaps the child has not yet really grasped the meaning of the separation. It would be a mistake to assume that because his feelings are not on the surface the child has already come to terms with the problem. If he does not understand or must repress an emotional experience now, the time will come when he must face it. The worker must be alert to this possibility so that he recognizes its manifestations later and is able to offer support to the child.

A worker, then, must watch and listen more than talk, for a child will lead the worker into areas where his problems lie. The most irrelevant story may lead, by association, back to an exceedingly relevant past event or person.

Even the fantasies a child produces recall the past. There is no need to ask, "What does this mean?" or "Why did you say that?" because the child probably cannot answer. However, if the worker waits, thoughts and feelings that seem out of context when first expressed will fall into place as he gets to know the child better. Some children chatter about useless information because they are overly anxious about revealing personal matters. As the child gains confidence in the worker this defense will be dropped.

The hardest child for workers to deal with is the one who remains silent. In such cases, the only feasible attitude to assume is a patient one that conveys the worker's willingness to wait.

HANDLING FEELINGS

Unless they have been severly hurt, most children will express their feelings. However, because of previous confusing life experiences and their very youthfulness, many children are not aware that their feelings are valid and appropriate. They will look at adults to validate their experience, just as a toddler who has taken a rough and frightening tumble may look to the adults caring for him, ready to cry but withholding tears until he learns if "big boys" cry. Many children coming to our care have had desperately painful emotional experiences, and have had to refrain from normal expression of pain and anger because of their experience with inhibiting adults. They need help from the social worker, including permission to express emotions appropriately.

Newer workers, fearing that they will be unable to control their feelings, sometimes approach emotional situations wrongly, with a stoically blank face. However, if the worker is angry, the child should see this in his face, hear it in his voice, and have it spoken of freely. The child will then see that the worker can, nevertheless, control his anger. The worker should help the child to free expressions by responding sympathetically to the emotion the child feels. If the child is sad, he should comfort him. If he is crying, he should hold him and provide loving comfort until the child is calmed. He should give the child a full measure of time to express his feelings. No child was ever hurt by seeing tears in a worker's eyes, if at the same time he knew that the worker had things under control.

On the other hand, if the child is angry and needs to heap hot coals upon his natural parent's head, the worker can permit this expression without joining in. The worker's sympathy for the child must stop short of judgmental attitudes toward the natural parents.

LIFE STORY BOOK

The use of visual aid in the treatment and care of children can be very helpful. If they can reconstruct an experience by playacting, visiting an actual location or person important in their past, or by seeing a picture of something that they remember, they will begin to correct false impressions of their past life. For this reason we begin to make a life story book for each child, at about age three when he becomes interested in himself and where he came from.

Our life story books are not to be confused with the "children's books" that we get together, beautifully photographed and nicely mounted, to be given to the adoptive family. The life story books are simply made, fingerprint-smudged epics, but they are working tools for understanding for the children and their workers. Their owners often take them to school, finding for the first time in eight or ten years of their lives that they can talk with authority about who they are and what their background is. The receptacle of all information that the worker has on the child and that the child is able to understand, the book is written, if possible in the child's own language. If the child is not able to write, we record his comments in his own language and then paste them in the scrapebook beside the appropriate pictures. For the child who has been in the care of more than one agency and has been moved from one foster home to another, the reconstruction of his life in a book like this becomes a tremendous emotional experience.

Children are not always anxious to begin such a book. Eddie, for example, was a child who had experienced two parental rejections in the past and had many unpleasant memories. He was most reluctant to begin a book about himself, because, as he said, "I don't want to remember."

I told Eddie that while there were many sad things he might like to forget, perhaps there were also pleasant things that he might want to remember. When Eddie insisted that he did not want a book and would not make any pictures for it, I told him that it would be important to him later and that we were going to buy the book. In the store, I had to take Eddie by the arm and steer him to the section where the scrapbooks were located. As Eddie looked at all the bright-colored books, his resistance lowered. He announced that he wanted "a sockadelic book" and then chose a large box of crayons, paste and construction paper. Later, when Eddie again assumed an attitude of resistance toward making pictures for his book, I insisted that if we were to go to the park, he must make at least one picture for his book before he could play on the equipment. Each session thereafter we made at least one picture for Eddie's book, and his resistance steadily decreased to a point where he would request materials to draw a picture and write delightfully spontaneous stories.

Never have I seen a prouder child than Eddie when adoptive placement day came and he could show the book to his new family. Today the book has a great deal of meaning for both Eddie and his adoptive parents.

VISITS

In addition to the life story books, visits can help children remember their past. Workers can plant images in their minds by taking them to visit a key place in their early childhood. Sometimes this is a house they remember vaguely, sometimes it is a cemetery where a parent or grandparent is buried . . . .

AGENCY ATOMSPHERE

We have tried to make the actual building and the noncasework staff become a part of an environment in which the older child will feel that he is valued by everyone involved in the process of finding a family for him.

Secretaries and receptionists with whom the children come in contact learn to recognize and call them by name. Each child is introduced to all of our adoption workers, and picnics are held for the purpose of helping children become acquainted with all staff members in a relaxed atmosphere.

The children also meet the supervisors responsible for the program, and become as comfortable in their company as they are with their workers. Sometimes a child needs to talk to a supervisor to understand a decision in his behalf, or when he is angry with his worker. For example, eight-year-old Bobby was a very outspoken child who had had two changes of workers and now was faced with a third. He rebelled and demanded to talk to the "boss." Miss B., the third social worker and a very sensitive woman, interrupted a conference in my office to say there was an angry young man outside my door who had something very important to discuss with me. I caught the urgency in her voice and admitted Bobby and the silent Miss B. Bobby looked me in the eye and told me in no uncertain terms about the other workers he had had, their promises of friendship, and how each had gone away. Since the workers had been honest with him, he knew that Mr. P., the second worker, was not leaving the agency but had been reassigned. He felt Miss B. might be nice but he liked Mr. P. and wanted to keep him.

I told Bobby that even before I assigned Miss B., I knew the change would be hard for him. It stunned Bobby to realize that I knew him so well when he had not noticed me at all. We discussed the earlier changes in detail until he remembered that each had been almost as hard in the beginning, that he had come to like each worker, and still considered them his friends. He became willing to try out Miss B. and left, promising to visit me again, which he has done many times.

SELECTING THE RIGHT FAMILY

In considering a family for an older child the usual criteria used for selecting families for infants must be expanded to include qualities having unique application to the needs of the older or hard-to-place child.

When our workers perceive that a family is interested in or has a particular talent for raising an older child, they explore the family's experiences and expectations in detail.

What kind of activities can the applicants visualize themselves engaged in with the child? Can they imagine ever allowing him to win an argument? What kind of child have they least enjoyed? Why? What do they especially like about their own children? What developmental period do they like best? Does their emotional tone reflect humor, anxiety, anticipation of enjoyment or fear of failure?

There are no right or wrong answers to these questions. The purpose of the inquiry is to find the child that would suit this family rather than reasons for removing the family from consideration. For instance, we discuss how they express affection. Placing a child who likes to be kissed in an undemonstrative family would only invite unhappiness and confusion, which is not to say that a reserved family is a bad family in which to raise a child. Or, again, what are the rules of the household and how are they made evident? Some families are verbal and direct, but many children also function well where rules are more subtly indicated.

We also consider how the child will react to the family's attitude about religion. For it would be confusing to place a youngster who has been taught to pray with a family that is indifferent to religion.

How the prospective family relates to serious emotional illness is another factor. Are they hung up on genetic purity—concepts of bad blood or bad seed—or sons inheriting the sins of the fathers? How steeped are they in these attitudes, if they exist? Can their concepts be broadened?

How much can they understand and enjoy the differences in children's personalities and leave them untouched? Some parents want children whose appearances and temperaments are similar to theirs. Some view the older child as totally moldable.

These families will either be disappointed or—what is more likely—the child will be bent and shaped in the form expected of him. A child's need for a permanent home is so strong that he may struggle to become the kind of person the family wants him to be. But the psychic price a child will pay if he is forced to change his personality patterns drastically is high.

Does the family recognize that the child's previous experiences are a part of him that should be added to, not blotted out? Can they be helped not to feel hurt by the child's references to other parental figures who he loved? If they have other children, do they know that they will not feel as close to the new child in exactly the same way that they feel close to their own chidren? If this is expected, the mature adult can accept the child in much the same way as he accepts the love of a new friend without expecting him to be like any previous friend.

PLACEMENT GUIDELINES

When we know a child well, and know that he understands the reality of his situation, when some of his unattractive behavior has been modified or subsided, and when we can predict with some confidence the child's response to a new home, we identify him as ready for adoptive placement. The child himself may be a long way from accepting the idea of new parents, but that does not deter us from including him in the agency's intensive parent search program.

We look for parents who have the capacity to understand what is going on within the child and are therefore able to guide him effectively by themselves. If a child can be sustained in a foster home, he certainly can be sustained in a permanent family if they understand his problems and have explored their ability to cope with them.

The selective process itself involves a team of staff members, including the child's worker and the applicant worker, who conduct an intensive review of all pertinent information concerning the child and the proposed family. Once the professional decision is made, the process breaks down into three phases: (1) telling the family and the child about each other; (2) arranging for the child to meet the family; and, (3) placement of the child. The details of implementing this rough plan, however, depend entirely upon the circumstances surrounding the placement, and it is generally the emotional tolerance of the child that determines the pace of events. Some children move slowly from the concept of a family "some day" to a family "now." In addition, a child's feelings toward his natural parents, apparently resolved, may resurface at the time of placement and have to be replayed and reunderstood. This final testing of defenses is a very healthy process and should not be confused with regression caused by anxiety.

When the child begins to show a genuine interest in the new family, it has been our experience that it is well to move as rapidly as possible. Once the child grasps the idea that this may be a new home for him, he should become as familiar as possible with the family before meeting them. This is a good time to show him photographs of the family and picutures of the house in which he may stay. It is during this tense period that the worker's total investment of time and emotional energy in the child should bear fruit. Despite glowing descriptions and promises of a beautiful future, it is only the child's knowledge of the worker's truthfulness, reliability, and concern for him that will enable him to accept on faith that this is the right family for him.

The child must not get the impression that he will have any effect on the choice of the adoptive family because it is not realistically possible for children to choose their own homes, and the child may become frightened if he thinks that his behavior can control the situation. If the child moves slowly in intense emotional situations, he should not be rushed beyond his capacity to cope with the experince.

In the course of the preplacement visit, the family should be helped to recognize aspects of the child's behavior that have been discussed with them previously. At this point, however, even the best of professional plans can still go awry. Human beings are so complex that there is no way of knowing definitely whether individuals, when they cast eyes upon each other, will take to each other warmly. Most of the time, if we have done our explorations well, we will have made a good "match." But there are times when it will be evident that the match will not work. A worker must be prepared for such an outcome, accept it, and handle the feelings of both child and family. It is important that the worker assume responsibility for the decision not to proceed with the placement and that he makes it clear to the child that the decision is his—not the parents'—in order to forestall the child's possible interpretation of the experience as another parental rejection.

If the match is a good one, the more quickly the child is moved into his new family situation, the better. Goodbyes in the foster home and in the child's neighborhood should be handled quickly and matter-of-factly so that their emotional level will remain within his tolerance. But goodbyes should never be omitted. By this time, too, the child should also begin to anticipate saying goodbye to the social worker.

SUPERVISING PLACEMENT

In our agency, the older child worker usually supervises placement since we anticipate that most problems will emanate from the child.

As the child continues supervision, it becomes absolutely essential for him to stop, reexamine his role, and refocus his entire approach to the new case situation. Continuing the same relationship he previously had with the child might be inappropriate and could interfere with the child's adjustment to the adoptive family. On the other hand, the relationship of the child worker to the child with residual problems should continue unaltered until the new family is able to take over the worker's role in helping the child understand the meaning and consequences of his behavior.

The worker might start by not seeing the child as often as before placement and gradually phase out one-to-one contact altogether. The worker must also be ready for the impact of his own feelings when he sees the child turning away from dependency upon him. One excellent worker, for instance, reported to her supervisor that she knew a case was going well, when she visited a little boy in his new adoptive home, Joey, who was playing in the yard, saw her and said, "Hi, you here?" and immediately ran to his new mother yelling, "Ma, can I have a glass of milk?"

12

OLDER CHILD ADOPTIVE PLACEMENT: A TIME OF FAMILY CRISIS

LINDA KATZ

The family crisis that inevitably follows the adoptive placement of an older child can be surmoumted if the social worker applies techniques based on crisis theory and family systems theory.

Placing an older child in adoption is a delicate and hazardous undertaking, and child welfare workers have learned to their sorrow that such placements can fail. The effect of a failed placement on a child is tragic, and the effect on the family similarly devastating. This paper proposes that placement workers look to two bodies of knowledge to provide new focus: family systems theory and crisis theory. Both these theories direct attention to the family as a whole, the family as a process, the family as a somewhat predictable set of emotions and reactions.

Certainly the placed child needs careful work prior to placement. But all too often work focuses primarily on the child. The social worker can easily narrow her view to the child's problems in the new family, in school, etc, and consequently limit her contacts with the family to their report on the child's adjustment to the family. Although she usually offers suggestions and support to the family, her attention is directed to the child and it is this tunnel vision that seriously weakens her effectiveness. Instead, her client should be "the family with a new child," which is to say, "the family in crisis."

In integrating aspects of crisis theory and family systems theory into sound thinking about older child placement, there will be unavoidable overlap. After all, the crisis occurs within the family system. However, the two theories are considered separately in this paper for purposes of clarity.

A SYSTEM FOCUS

The child is a new family member whose arrival will disrupt an established system of relationships. The worker must convey, long before the placement, that this disruption is normal and predictable—what every family experiences when a major change takes place within it. During the adoption study she helps the family assess the current family system for strengths and vulnerable areas. For instance, who will lose his or her accustomed place in the family hierarchy? Will the family's youngest child now become an older sibling? What ties now exist between the siblings? Who now shares a bedroom? What chores are assigned to what person and how might that change? What are the father's ties to each child now? What does the mother find most rewarding about her role now? What is most exasperating? In this process the worker and family together can decide about the family's readiness for an older child placement, based on awareness of what this could mean to the family. With this foundation laid early, much fruitful work can be done after placement, when the system is under stress.

HEMEOSTASIS

A primary concept to be taught to families is that of hemeostasis, or balance. Every family has established a balance of relationships. Whenever a family member leaves or a new one enters, this balance is upset and a new balance must be gradually reestablished after a period disturbing equilibrium. Moreover, the new balance will be different from the old.

Satir uses the analogy of a mobile in explaining hemeostasis (2:119). Everyone in the current family is in a different place, suspended by a string of a different length, yet there is balance. When the new child is attached in a new place on the mobile, everyone swings wildly around, losing his or her comfortable place.

For example, in an adopting family with two natural sons, the entrance of a eight-year-old adopted daughter will have profound and permanent effects on the relationship between the two boys, between husband and wife, and between each child and each parent. Some of the changes will be pleasant. The mother will enjoy outlines with their new daughter; the father will be proud of his daughter's growing affection for him. But the boys will receive less attention from their parents; the mother may be jealous of her husband's attachment to the little girl; the father may chafe at new demands on him at home. Added to these tensions is the emotional disturbance of the older child placed for adoption. The child is often expert at picking the tender spots of the new family's system, ecouraging destructive alliances, and acting out. All of these things the family must think out in advance, with the worker's support.

> The Rs, a childless couple, had an affectionate, mature relationship. Any differences were handled calmly and reasonably. With the placement of Donald, age ten, their methods of handling friction and anger began to fail, and Donald's angry outbursts reverberated through the marital relationship. Both the Rs used the worker frequently for help in dealing with rage and helplessness.
>
> The Ms were pleased that their three natural children had always been well behaved, responding to firm but usually unspoken parental expectations. When Sheila was placed, at age eight, such subtleties became ineffectual. Sheila was accustomed to strict verbal and physical discipline that was uncomfortable for the Ms. For example, a casual request from Mr. M, "Sheila, would you mind setting the table?" brought the response, "I don't want to." Such failures in communication did not represent rebellion, but rather clashing of two established systems. (If I'm really supposed to set the table, he'll yell at me to do it, and then I'll know.") The worker had to help the whole family examine their expectations, and make changes to incorporate Sheila.

When the worker treats this complex mix of factors as a family problem, rather than as the child's problem, she helps the family's previously healthy system reassert itself in a new form, incorporating a new member. Everyone's feelings are carefully considered, all the family members received encouragement, and the family's efforts to cope with the disequilibrium are supported by the worker.

FAMILY PAIN

A second useful concept offered by Satir is that when one family member has pain, all other members feel it in some way. Moving into a new family is certainly painful to the child (even if the move is desired). When the child shows this by tears, depression, or withdrawal, other family members may be surprised to find similar feelings in themselves, memories reawakened, or a sudden wish to deny such painful thoughts. If the new child is mourning the loss of previous parents, the adoptive family may feel threatened or resentful. If the child has outbursts of crying, other children in the family may break into tears also. If the child shows his or her pain by fighting, rejecting the new family, running away, etc., other family members may be frightened by their own angry impulses, want to punish the child or suppress his feelings. No one is isolated from the child's strong feelings; hence the worker's attention is one the family as a whole, their day-to-day mood, irritations, disappointments, successes. The worker must impress upon the family that these times will be not only distressing but even tumultuous. In spite of their desire to provide a happy home for the child, they cannot expect sainthood from themselves.

There are some common issues in older child placement that can lead to extreme negative feelings in the family, upsetting the homeostasis so severely that the child is excluded. These include sexual acting out or provocative language, the child's use of the "ghosts" of his previous parents to wound the new parents, the child's withdrawal into a cold and unresponsive shell, leaving the new family feeling rejected. The family's reactions are so extremely difficult for most adoptive parents to reveal to the worker that it is well worth it for the worker to introduce these subjects whenever it seems appropriate.

If the worker is concentrating her attention primarily on the newly placed child, it is difficult for the family to use the worker to help with their own feelings of outrage. They can come to believe that their negative feelings are not normal, to feel quilty over their anger and to develop fears about possible failure of the placement. If they do not see the placing worker as really their worker, they may block communication about these feelings, thereby exacerbating the problems. Thus, the worker must open up these areas for sympathetic scrutiny prior to placement. She must then keep them open after placement so the new family system that finally results can be strong, based on openness and respect for feelings. One way the worker teaches these systems concepts is by seeing the whole family together, during the adoption study and thereafter. Family interviews are a rich source of learning both for the work and the family. Of course, talking privately with the parents about vital placement issues is often appropriate, and can complement family sessions.

CRISIS INTERVENTION

The term "crisis" can be defined as a sudden change in one's life that imposes heavy demands, stretches one's resources too far, and threatens loss of security or self-esteem. Of course, placement is always a crisis for the placed child, but families must be made aware that they, too, will feel "in crisis" and that is predicatable. Fortunately, unlike many other kinds of crisis that families confront, placement gives them the opportunity to prepare for the experience, with the help of a social worker. Depending on how the crisis is dealt with, the family will be strengthened or weakened in its functioning.

IMPORTANCE OF INTERVENTION

The outcome of a crisis experience is not necessarily determined by the person's previous personal strength, but, rather, by the kind of help (or lack of it) he or she receives during the crisis (1:53). Placement workers have to feel confident that potential adoptive families come to this challenge with substantial strength and health, but then the emphasis shifts to what the worker can offer as the current drama unfolds.

Typically, a crisis has a time limit of four to six weeks, after which it is resolved in either a healthy or unhealthy way. The placement worker can learn a vital lesson from this—in older child adoption her most intensive work must be done in the first weeks or months following placement. This is not to underrate the importance of careful preparation prior to placement; both efforts are essential. Crisis theory also teaches that people are most amenable to intervention at the point of crisis. Even a short delay in offering help allows defenses to spring up. This immediate openness to help allows the worker to make the greatest impact at the time of placement; thereafter, her influence will lessen.

In practical terms, crisis theory puts many demands on the worker during that early period. To be fully knowledgeable and helpful, she should be a part of the initial placement visiting between the child and the family, or have contact with the family on each of those days. She must focus on the details of what happened from the family's point of view, explore their individual feelings about the child and their inner turmoil over the risks of this impactful experience. She must allow the family to participate fully in the decision-making process. Once the child is placed the in-person contacts should remain frequent, even during the expected "honeymoon" period. These contacts should be at least weekly, with supplementary phone contacts every few days. In some cases, the worker will come to the family's home; in others, she will see them in her office. To encourage them to keep her in touch with day-to-day developments, her home phone number should be given. Interviews may often last two hours or more. This is not to say, however, that the family's autonomy is surrendered in favor of the worker's expertise. A large part of the casework responsibility at this time is identifying and supporting the family's own coping mechanisms, reminding them of progress they have made with the child, and looking forward with them to what can be expected.

As each family member copes with the day-to-day stresses of the new child's placement, there will be a rising and falling tension. At some points the family member will feel a need to deny the tension, and seek escape. At other times they will confront it and work on it. The worker must be sensitive to this, not forcing the issue but seeing it in perspective herself. One day she may hear "Oh, everything has really settled down here! I'm sure the worst is over." The following day it may well be: "I don't know what's happening to all of us. I've never seen our family so out of sorts."

Adoption workers who have placed troubled older children often have noticed that sometime in the months after placement a family that has always been so open and welcoming is drawing away from the worker, phoning less often, and in general being less involved with her. Far from being disturbing, this is a signal that the crisis itself is ending disturbing, this is a signal that the crisis itself is ending and the family is once more operating independently, now with a new member. At this point the worker's greatest influence is ending, and her role is becoming less exacting. Indeed, the normal family's self-esteem does not permit strong dependency on a long-term basis.

At any point in the postplacement stage, groupwork can be beneficial, as it permits families to gain support from each other. Even when the major placement crisis ends, many difficulties remain (e.g., regressions, anniversary reactions), with which the family may need help. Thus, casework continues throughout the postplacement period, and the groupwork can be a valuable supplement. A group of families all of whom have adopted older children offers a forum for parents to report successes as well as frustrations, with a common bond of understanding.

REFERENCES

Caplan, Gerald. *Principles of Preventive Psychiatry.* New York: Basic Books, 1964.
Satir, Virginia. *Peoplemaking.* Palo Alto, California: Science and Behavior Books, 1972.

13

TREATMENT OF LATENCY-AGE ADOPTED CHILDREN AND PARENTS

MATILDA T. BELLUCCI

A group therapy program enables adopted children and their parents to share these feelings. The children involved in this program were age nine to thirteen and had experienced at least five foster placements. The staff concluded that the program did meet some of the needs of this group.

In social work, professionals frequently encounter an older child who has been surrendered for adoption. Special home-finding, preparation, and placement are demanding work, but they are only the beginning steps if the adoptions of these often disturbed and disturbing children are to be viable.

The adoptive staff of the family, children, and adult services division of Hamilton County Welfare Department in Cincinnati, Ohio, initiated group treatment for newly placed adopted children, nine to thirteen years old, who had experienced at least five foster home placements, with all the suffering and damage entailed in such moves. These children were only beginning to let themselves experience security-giving primary relationships. One may question the term *latency* for this particular group; they had not had the continuing parental relationships considered necessary to resolve prelatency conflicts.

RATIONALE FOR GROUP TREATMENT

Social agencies have long been aware of the difficulties involved in providing services after a child's adoption. To minimize these problems, the department's adoption staff used the services of staff members who were not involved in adoption work and would, therefore, be less threatening and more conducive to openness. The group treatment modality was thought more promising than traditional individual supervision or family treatment. Groups are generally considered appropriate for children in latency. The support and confrontation so accessible in groups would prove more acceptable, not only to latency-aged children but to the adopting parents. Futhermore, feelings become more accessible when shared. The initial motivation came from a thirteen-year-old boy who wanted to share his experiences with others placed adoptively late in life. With this rationale, referrals rapidly ensued. A child's need instigated the children's group, and one parent's similar feelings prompted the formation of a parent's group. It began to meet during the children's second session and was also led by nonadoption staff.

In assessing the need for these services, the staff had tentatively proposed short-term groups *of six to ten conventional one-hour treatment sessions.* What had not been anticipated were the enthusiasm of most of the families and the responsiveness of the children. These factors amended the initial contract; groups continued for fourteen sessions before adjourning for several weeks of summer vacation.

THE CHILDREN

Records on the children provided meaningful themes and shared experiences for the group. Except for one child who had had one last preplacement week of foster care, all children had been in their adoptive homes for months; one adoption had been completed legally.

In order to minimize anxiety, screening visits with each child and a parent were undertaken within two weeks before the group's proposed beginning. The adoption staff had well prepared these parents, who were mostly professional, middle-class whites. No authoritative pressures were used. Although undoubtedly tacitly threatened by such intervention, the parents seemed willing to assume risk in order to ease the child's and their own pain. Several parents had had earlier gratifying group experiences.

No one was screened out; those accepted consisted of the *two oldest* (a girl aged nine and a boy of ten) of three siblings placed with a childless couple; a boy aged twelve, placed with a single-parent father; two thirteen-year-old boys placed with families who had their own children; and a nine-year-old boy whose stability was threatened by the recent placement with his adoptive parents of his two-year-old sister.

In an attempt to achieve some balance for the one girl in the group, staff members tried to include another girl, whose adoptive family had been her foster family for over five years. During this time, they had resisted agency contact and any other indication that the child was not their natural child. The child enjoyed a few sessions, but the family became so threatened by the possibility of opening painful areas that they withdrew. This is a major adoption issue—a child's need for a particular home, belatedly assessed as disturbed and disturbing, and the family's resistance to modification. The adoption was completed even though the agency was aware that this step prepared the child for heightened turmoil in adolescence, if not sooner.

CHILDREN'S THEMES IN THERAPY

As anticipated, the children had much in common. Immediate and continuing areas of comfortable verbalization concerned experiences in emergency receiving centers and foster homes, all of which they shared at different or, in some instances, at the same times. They all had had significant people in their lives; above all, they shared the same fears of rejection and feelings of pain. For the first few sessions, they focused on past experiences, and subsequently increasing emhasis was placed on present ones.

They readily talked about their natural families. Those who had known their natural families had vivid memories; even the most violent of them were shared with relish. Those children surrendered at birth understood why intellectually, but remained puzzled that their mothers knew so quickly that they did not want their babies.

An early theme was the children's confusion. Despite the adoption staff's elaborate efforts to recreate the past, most of the children did not know the number of foster homes in which they had been placed. Many had two first names, most had used successive foster family surnames. Even the public schools had not been able to systematize this name useage. Three of the boys felt they were wanted primarily to continue the adoptive family's name. Only one boy had been able to discuss this feeling with his mother, whose denial he still disbelived. Feelings about names continued relatively unabated even after adoption, for several children kept their natural family's surname as their middle name.

At one time, group leaders speculated that those children who had known their own parents and who had been released by them could move more easily into new relationships than those released at birth. One child, surrendered at birth and placed for adoption soon after, seemed less able to resolve these past losses. When asked about this tendency, another boy, surrendered for adoption after several years, stated that it seemed best to him to be surrendered at birth, for then a person need not know that he was adopted. He was immediately confronted on the need to know. Others also felt, however, that knowing and losing one's natural parents was more painful than never knowing them. Throughout the group meetings, staff reiterated their position that adoptive parents are additions to, not replacements for, natural parents.

Feelings of being unwanted persisted. Several children felt wanted only for their labors, a feeling undoubtedly related to rural foster home placement. "Up for adoption" felt like "up for auction"; they thought they had no options and felt like "slaves." This emotion was also expressed in the conviction of some adoptees that their families had wanted a child of the other sex. No one could want them for themselves.

In addition, the children felt omnipotent: They had caused marital trouble, divorce, even deaths in their foster homes. While sharing their opinions on this subject, they confronted each other on the unreality of their presumed their foster homes. While sharing their opinions on this subject, they confronted each other on the unreality of their presumed omnipotence.

They related their acting-out behavior during the sessions to what they called "attention-getting." They denied that such activity was testing, although they were familiar with this seemingly parental word. Attention-getting proved useful early in enabling them to secure minimal control over each other. Except in isolated instances, their control of each other's behavior was the major control; only once was one member's temporary exclusion tentatively suggested. The staff used early adjournment when contagious restlessness dictated such a move; however, the full hour was committed to verbal group treatment, whether informally with a few members or with the whole group.

Another theme the children tackled with gusto was sibling rivalry—totally unrelated to whether the sibling was natural or adoptive. There was evidenced a deep feeling of being second-rate, of not belonging. With the almost constant depreciation of each other by the two natural siblings in the group, members and leaders had an example of a here-and-now confrontation. This brother and sister were confronted on how such baiting upset others and how difficult it must be for their adoptive mother. Knowledge of rivalrous feelings in others made this group less uncomfortable with their own. In an attempt to discover if the children ever felt enough gratification, a question was asked related to the amount of treats they were given; several children said they never received enough. As uncomfortable as these feelings were, they had to endure them.

Anger was always an underlying theme and feeling, under scoring their experiences. Handling their anger was an overt agenda item—one they picked up themselves later without further direction. Many examples of acting-out and withdrawing were cited, including destruction of property, stealing, and running away. This discussion probably led, in turn, to greater comfort about their shared angry feelings which they became more able to verbalize. Their needs were also being met more adequately in their new adoptive homes; they had more options for sublimation, such as noncompetitive sports, music, and other areas of noncompulsory activity.

This topic leads to a seemingly important insight. As commendable as most foster families are, their expectations of and demands upon their children are not the same as those of more academically oriented, culturally enriched adoptive families. From homes in which academic standards were minimal, these children moved to teaching, striving parents and professional and even intellectual families. While latency-aged children in general manage to adapt to the enormous, and often seemingly arbitrary, demands society places upon them, the children in this group must have been only intellectually prepared for the different expectations of their new worlds. Although the families themselves were undoubtedly primed to minimize these discrepancies, their life-styles excluded difference—a predominant feeling for all foster children. Language was only one minor area, but one where the difference quickly became evident, and this restriction further lessened these children's already limited ability to talk. One ten-year-old's major activity with his father was chess; he had no avowed disinterest in this activity, only commenting that he never won. Examples came readily. These ordinarily sensitive parents took for granted their life-styles, which at times were worlds apart from those of their adoptive children, who so desperately needed to gratify parents, teachers, scout leaders, and other regimenting adults in their social worlds.

At times, some of the children expressed a longing for their former, more undemanding placements where it had been less important to meet parental demands and gain acceptance, and where they had been more able to gratify their own wishes. These children had been "rescued," but they did not always feel that the change was an unmixed blessing. Adoption is an adult device to meet the child's undeniable right to a family; the older child, however, retains mixed feelings.

Another engrossing topic introduced during the eleventh session was sex. The only girl in the group was at camp, but the boys denied that her absence triggered their ability to talk. Talk they did, with many basic questions. Language was a barrier; they could make themselves understood, but not in language acceptable to their new worlds. Nevertheless, they were committed to learning with minimal silliness. The older children did not feel that such discussion was premature for the younger ones; they had been curious when younger and had wanted such an outlet. Masturbation was openly and freely discussed. One intellectualizing twelve-year-old commented that his foster parents would have threatened "twenty years' hard labor" just for mentioning it. If sex is such a conflict-ridden area during latency, as most child welfare authorities suggest, the openness and freedom of group interaction must have alleviated some of this emotion.

Sex did subside as a major focus during the thirteenth session when the group's girl and her brother returned from camp, and the child most interested went to camp. With adjournment imminent and camping absences intermittent, it became increasing difficult to attain any focus.

PARENT GROUP SESSIONS

Without any screening or background material, the parents' group leader began short-term, content-oriented sessions with five parents. Three of them were or had been teachers—a common bond for them as well as for their children. For the children, this fact provided possibilities for Critical Parent—Not OK Child transactions.

Techniques were support, clarification, interpretation, and some teaching. Each week, the leader read a summarized account of the children's sessions and wherever possible followed the general themes. This dictated summary was fundamental in making the children's general feelings available to the astonished parents, but maintained the children's confidentiality. It also helped maintain interstaff communication which was never a problem.

Generally, the parents focused on themselves as persons and on insights gained since their children's placement. They wanted specific advice in helping their children and themselves; the group process, however, did not remain at this level. Rather, their feelings about themselves, their needs for children, and their expectations came to the foreground.

Motivation for adoption was primarily the need for a family with cohesiveness and integrity. Altruism prevailed in their humanitarianism. In one instance, a depressive reaction seemed evident; this parent's expectations for a child were finally becoming a reality and the change in life-style exposed the parent to constant exasperation. The children generally were not changing as the parents had expected, despite all their efforts. Furthermore, the community itself was not understanding of the miniscule growth rate for these children. Other parents, teachers, and relatives found the families just as lacking as the adoptive parents must have felt.

Their feelings of responsibility for changing their charges were basic to their expectations: What if these children did not, could not, respond according to the parents' educational, social, and emotional expectations? Getting in touch with these feelings was an important group function, helping to relieve the burden of responsibility and to add some reality to their rescue fantasies. Basic to these fantasies was the parents' conviction that their home environment would change the child according to their expectations.

Although the adoptive parents rejected their child's past—and at times the disturbing child himself—they were only intellectually prepared for the child's resistance to and rejection of them. These emotions seemed almost more than they could tolerate, but the professional staff marveled at the deep commitment these families maintained under such stress, a commitment essential to successful adoption of older children.

The parents themselves wanted continuing services after the completion of adoption. They attended group meetings even when the children were at camp. Fathers participated whenever possible. Before the sixth and after the fourteen and final session of the series, parents were offered options of terminating or continuing after the vacation. Only one mother did not return after adjournment.

CONCLUSION

Social welfare's mandate to insure every child a home imposes weighty responsibilities on agencies who find themselves with older children in need of adoption, and on the communities which provide the homes and fund the agencies. As suggested in this article, home-finding and placement are only the beginning steps if such services are to function well. An agency's responsibility for continuing support and clarification seems clear, particularly when the community and other supportive sources are no longer as understanding or concerned.

Group composition requires more definitive screening for set and stage balance. These children were in two different stages of latency. The younger ones were more obedient and less aggressive; their interest levels were pregenital. The three older boys were more rebellious and independent, verging on adolescence both chronologically and emotionally. Lack of balance may have impeded group bonds, particularly for the only girl. These children's feelings about the past were similar, but their present thrusts very different.

Currently, two such balanced groups are being started. Girls, who seem to be placed in adoption earlier, predominate in the younger group, and only boys are accepted in the older. Staff shortages have temporarily precluded reorganization of the parents' group. This lack has caused a severe handicap for those parents requesting service and has prevented communication of the children's concerns and feelings, which now have less access for feedback. The lessened degree of feedback severely limits this service's effectiveness. Pending the formation of another parents' group, some way must be found to provide feedback while maintaining the children's trust and confidentiality.

In conclusion, the group modality does seem to meet some of the needs of these vulnerable parents and children. The professionals involved now wonder at their belated awakening to these needs.

6

14

TREATMENT OF A TWO-YEAR-OLD IN PREPARATION OF ADOPTION

MARTHA J. WARFIELD

A moving account is given of a relationship in which a caseworker and a young boy share a wide range human emotions and experiences as a very frightened child is prepared for adoption.

Rusty became my client when the worker who had known him since birth left the Jewish Family and Children's Service. Our first meeting occurred when I picked up Rusty and his foster mother for a trip to the agency pediatrician. My impression of Rusty that February day was of a tiny boy, solemn and shy, who eyed me surreptitiously with big brown eyes from the safety of his foster mother's lap. It was a cold day, and, swathed in an oversized snowsuit, Rusty looked even tinier and younger than his twenty months. As I drove Rusty to his appointment, little did I suspect that this meeting marked the beginning of a relationship in which I was to share with him a wide range of human emotions and experiences.

At the start of our relationship my very presence came to symbolize a dreaded visit to yet another medical facility. I soon felt, but could not ease, his terror and desolation at hospitalization and separation from the foster family with whom he had lived since birth. Later, as we began to work toward adoption, ours became a relationship in which I shared in the rebuilding of Rusty's trust in the world beyond his immediate foster family, and in his growing sense of autonomy and developing confidence in his right to be an individual with feelings and impulses of his own. At the end of our relationship, I was further privileged to participate in the uniting of this child, whom I had grown to know and to love, with an adoptive family which was able both to give love and to respect Rusty's need to accept love and return it at his own pace.

MEDICAL PROBLEMS OF CHILD

At the first encounter in our seven months together, we saw Rusty's pediatrician, who had entered the case when Rusty was thirteen months old. At the time the agency had become concerned and confused by Rusty's multiplicity of physical symptoms. There had been a one-sided paralysis noted by the foster mother and by the agency's preadoptive prediatrician at Rusty's first routine checkup when he was one month old. With the help of exercises and massages given by the foster mother, this paralysis improved so much that by the time Rusty was thirteen months old, the original stiffness, weakness, and physical asymmetry were no longer visible, even to the trained eye. During this period of time, Rusty had been seen three times by a pediatric neurologist and twice by a child psychologist in order to evaluate the extent of neurological damage, and to help the agency predict whether the child would develop normally or whether his needs would continue to be special. It was the psychologist who first noted the extreme caution and reserve with which Rusty reacted to new situations, and who guessed that his intellectual potential was greater than the infant's tests suggested. These repeated invasions of Rusty's physical, mental, and emotional space by prying and probing hands, instruments, and voices, although necessary did nothing to increase his confidence in himself and in the world around him.

If this early paralysis had been Rusty's only problem, in all probability he would have been adopted long before we met. However, Rusty also had a feeding problem. He had been a small baby, weighing less than five pounds at birth. He was fined boned and likely always to be small like his natural parents. However, his low birth-weight in addition to the stiffness made him difficult to feed and aroused the anxiety of his foster mother. Rusty gagged on anything solid or lumpy, and continued eating strained infant food long past the age when most babies enjoy finger foods and the experience of feeding themselves. More important, after rejecting his bottle at the age of nine months, Rusty became apparently unable to swallow liquids, choking and coughing after the first few sips. His weight gain between twelve and eighteen months was minimal.

The swallowing problem and the failure to gain weight caused continuing anxiety in his foster mother and puzzled his doctors, who wondered if there was some connection between his swallowing difficulties and the earlier paralysis. Several tentative medical diagnoses were explored and ruled out. When he was fifteen months old, Rusty had undergone a barium x-ray; the liquid barium had been poured into him through a tube. The test proved negative, for the suspected medical conditions but further undermined his faith in mankind—especially, one may conjecture, in social workers and doctors. At this point, it was decided to let nature take its course; it was hoped that Rusty would continue to gain weight, however slowly, and would "outgrow" his swallowing problem.

Unfortunately, on the day of our first meeting and the visit to the doctor, it was discovered that Rusty was losing weight. Hospitalization for more exhaustive evaluation was scheduled for the following week. By the time of his discharge two weeks later, several facts about Rusty had become apparent to those who were responsible for his care. The first was that there was no discernible organic basis for his inability to swallow. The second fact was that this inability to swallow was selective. With some people, Rusty could drink a cup of juice quite nicely; with others he choked, sputtered, and managed to get more juice on his clothing and on the floor than in himself. These two things about Rusty were encouraging; the third was not.

Hospitalization with its attendant separation from home and the nightmare of repeated examinations and tests had severely traumatized Rusty, increasing his natural reserve and caution to an almost catatonic immobility in the presence of strangers. Rusty was now twenty-one months old, cleared for adoption from a physical point of view, but with emotional disturbances ranging from a psychogenic feeding problem to severe separation anxiety manifested by extreme withdrawal and lethargy when away from his foster home. The agency had two tasks at this time. One was to find adoptive parents who would take an older child with a medical history such as Rusty's. This task belonged to the agency's adoptive worker. The other was mine—the preparation of Rusty for leaving his foster home and entering his adoptive home.

CASEWORK TO STRENGTHEN TRUST

Following his return from the hospital, I began to work with Rusty and his foster mother to heal the emotional wounds caused by our attempts to understand and deal with his physical ills. The swallowing problem had begun to improve while Rusty was still in the hospital; with reasurance from both me and the pediatrician, the foster mother became a bit more relaxed about what Rusty did and did not drink, and allowed him more control over when and how much he wanted to drink. With his daily food and liquid intake less of a battleground, Rusty slowly began to gain the weight he had lost.

The fear of leaving home and the fear of strange people and places proved a much more complex problem to deal with. Five months before his adoptive placement, I slowly began to build a relationship with Rusty that was strong enough and secure enough to serve as the bridge to his new home. I began by visiting in the foster home twice a week, talking to the foster mother , and playing with his foster sister. Rusty learned that my appearance did not necessarily mean a trip to the doctor. His initial tendency was to disappear into another room or behind a curtain whenever I appeared. However, Rusty's natural curiosity and exuberance were strong, and he began to approach me, first visually then physically. Within three weeks he was bringing books to me for him to "read" and was showing off his skills, which ranged from piano "playing" and singing to turning somersaults and riding on his kiddie car.

At this point I decided it was time to expand our horizons. Our first trip away from his foster home, was from my point of view, a disaster. We took a short ride to a nearby shopping center where Rusty had been many times before with his foster family. Being in the car with me did not seem to bother him because he always loved to go for rides. However, once in the store he was petrified and clung to my neck like a baby monkey clinging to its mother. The ice cream cone I offered as a treat was not even tasted; it melted and dripped over both of us as Rusty clung to me and stared wildly at all strangers as if their very presence was an invasion. There was one positive aspect of the trip; Rusty apparently decided that even if I was rather frightening, the rest of the world was worse. Or he may have resigned himself to the fact that I was bigger and more powerful than he and did have control over where we went together.At any rate, this experience marked the beginning of his acceptance of his trips with me.

We now began a series of semiweekly trips to the agency, both for the therapeutic value of the time with me and with the hope that the agency would become a comfortable place for Rusty. We could then use the agency as home base in his transfer to his new family. The first agency visit was discouraging. Although Rusty left his foster home without protest, he ignored me during the twenty-minute drive, stubbornly looking out the window and ignoring my comments about where we were going, what we were going to do,and what was to be seen on our route.

Once at the agency, I took Rusty into the playroom. There he became completely immobile, standing rooted to the spot where I had put him down, one hand on my knee, beseeching me with his big brown eyes to take him away. None of the proffered toys interested him in the slightest.

I had hoped that Rusty would begin to form a relationship with the adoption worker who would supervise his placement, but, it was quickly apparent that it would be a long time before Rusty formed a relationship with anyone. We realized that Rusty needed considerable time to relax and to rebuild his trust in people before we could hope to place him successfully in an adoptive home. Fortunately, the needed time was provided by the fact that it took several months for the adoption worker to find the right family.

Subsequent visits to the agency began as repeat performances of the first visit, with the initial, almost catatonic imobility. I felt that the closed playroom we had used on the first visit was somehow threatening to Rusty, so we moved into the glass-enclosed children's waiting room. Working with Rusty there was somewhat like working in a fishbowl. It was disconcerting to me, but the glass walls enabled Rusty to see and be exposed to a variety of people while maintaining the distance he so desperately needed. With each visit Rusty's initial immobility lasted a shorter time, and we began to develop a pattern of play which was the basis of my therapeutic work with Rusty. I felt that there were two intertwined areas of development with which I could help Rusty. The first task was to strengthen his sense of trust which had been so badly shaken by his traumatic medical experiences and separation. The second was to help develop and strengthen Rusty's sense of work as an autonomous individual. Along with this task went the related aim of developing Rusty's sense of mastery over his environment, which had been decimated by his experience of being a helpless victim of both men and machines.

We worked on these problems in several ways. To increase his trust I had to prove trustworthy. It is difficult to know how much a two-year-old, especially a very nonverbal two-year-old, understands; nevertheless, I was careful always to explain to Rusty where we were going and what we were going to do. If the situation varied from the usual or was in some other way strange to Rusty, I verbalized for Rusty both the strangeness and his possible feelings about it. I offered reassurance, but never without first identifying the elements which created apprehension and then naming the feelings aroused. At the same time I communicated my confidence in him and in his ability to master each new situation as it arose.

We worked concurrently on developing Rusty's sense of worth as an autonomous individual. Development of a sense of mastery played an important part in this work. In the past he had tried to master his environment in a negative way which had proved self-destructive. He had tried to assert himself with his foster mother by refusing to swallow. He had a chance with me to experience his own autonomy in a more positive fashion. Rusty himself showed me the way in which to reach him. During our second visit to the playroom he handed me a toy telephone, indicated that I should talk. For nearly forty minutes I kept up a one-sided conversation over this toy telephone, describing Rusty's activities as he wandered around the waiting room, touching and examining toys and equipment. At the end of this visit, Rusty took the telephone home with him. This pattern continued throughout our work together; after each visit a different toy went home and was carefully returned the next visit.

I also felt that for some reason Rusty had missed out on the experience of mutuality and reciprocity between mother and infant, which is so vital to the child's development of a sense of himself as a separate individual. This reciprocity is ordinarily manifested in the peek-a-book and patty-cake games that begin toward the end of the first year, and in the reciprocal feeding of mother and child—"a bite for me and a bite for you." Rusty's physical needs had been met in his foster home, but I suspected that they had been met on his foster mother's schedule rather than on Rusty's. I also suspected that any of his attempts to feed her a bite of cookie, for instance, or to share a newly found but slightly dirty treasure would have been rejected.

In his relationship with me, Rusty had his chance both to tell me what to do and to share with me experiences and physical objects. A table and set of chairs were in the playroom. Rusty delighted in telling me in which chair to sit. As he played around the room, I sat watching him and commenting on his play. He occasionally came up to me and indicated by pointing that I was to move to a different chair. As I did so, he grinned delightedly. During each visit he moved me at least half a dozen times. No particular reason for the moves was evident. I felt that he merely like to be boss and thoroughly enjoyed his sense of power. Rusty also delighted in feeding me. As he grew braver, we used part of our visits to wander through the hallways of the agency. This petite brown-eyed charmer with the solemn expression quickly won the hearts of the rest of the staff. Rusty disliked being touched and would step backward to avoid physical contact. However, he was not averse to accepting a piece of candy, a pretzel, a lump of sugar. After returning to the playroom with our booty, Rusty solemnly shared his goodies with me, laughing with pleasure as I popped a piece of candy into my mouth or chewed, with much lip smacking, a lump of his sugar. Any leftovers were carefully taken home.

By this time I was encouraged by Rusty's progress in our relationship. I felt that his shyness and reserve were understandable in view of his traumatic background and somewhat repressive environment. I sspected that part of his shyness was constitutional. However, from the point of view of placing this child in an adoptive home, there was still the nagging question of whether he could react positively to new parents quickly enough to sustain their interest and investment in him. During the time that I was working with Rusty, the adoptive worker was calling many families known to the agency to attempt to find suitable parents who were interested in this child. Most adoptive parents want newborn babies, and by this time Rusty was over two. By a quirk of fate, those families who were willing to consider an older child with a history of medical problems were all interested in having girls. At this time we felt that we should look beyond Jewish Family and Children's Service. Consequently, at the age of twenty-six months Rusty was placed on the state adoption exchange register so that we would have the benefit of a larger pool of prospective parents. The adoption exchange had on their register only one family of the same religious faith as Rusty, and their needs and his were not compatible.

While continuing our search for parents, we felt the need for a final consultation about Rusty. I felt that his therapeutic gains with me were quite substantial, but we were still concerned about this immobility when he was out of his foster home. Like previous consultants, the child psychiatrist who observed Rusty agreed that his intellectual potential was at least average, but he was concerned that Rusty's unresponsiveness was severe enough to discourage adoptive parents. However, since the picture of Rusty at home—vibrant, energetic, and enthusiastic—and the picture in the agency—apathetic, dejected, and unmoving—were so different, we decided to trust Rusty and continue our search for parents. Shortly thereafter, the persistent search of the adoption worker was rewarded. She had found for Rusty not only parents but two brothers and a sister.

ACQUAINTANCE WITH ADOPTIVE FAMILY

The process of meeting and getting to know Rusty's new parents, sister, and brothers was spread over a three-week period. During these three weeks there were seven visits between Rusty and his new family, with Rusty becoming more involved each time. Ordinarily visits between children and prospective parents take place in the agency. In Rusty's care, we had become convinced that his fear of all institutions extended to the agency building and was a factor in his tendency to withdraw and close up whenever he entered the agency. Because of this fact and because it was easier for him to relate to other children than to adults, we decided to have Rusty meet his new family in the more natural setting of their home.

On the day of the first visit, the adoption worker drove Rusty and me to his new home, where he was eagerly awaited by Mr. and Mrs. Roseman and their three children: Jonathan (eleven), Debby (seven), and Eric (four). During this initial visit Rusty was understandably shy and tense and clung to me tenaciously at first. However, by the end of the visit he had gone to his new mother and had begun to relax in her lap as they sat and rocked and looked at a picture book. He was interested in the children and watched them intently, but he was too fearful to become actively involved. Rusty's experience with men had been mostly at the wrong end of some sort of medical instrument, and he had apparently concluded that all men were doctors. Consequently, Rusty seemed determined to avoid Mr. Roseman and accepted him much more slowly than the other members of the family. Fortunately, his father-to-be possessed the maturity and understanding to let Rusty come to him on his own terms and at his own pace.

The second visit was also conducted in the Roseman home, but with only Mrs. Roseman and Eric present. We felt that Rusty had probably been a bit overwhelmed during the first visit, and we wanted to give him time to adapt to the new situation and get to know the family members in a less concentrated fashion. Rusty again demonstrated that he was comfortable with Mrs. Roseman who was marvelously attuned to a child's needs. Like Mr. Roseman she respected Rusty's need to develop a relationship at his own pace. At the same time, she was able to inspire his confidence in her and in the rightness of what was taking place.

Two days later Rusty and I again spent the morning at the Roseman home with the whole family present. Mr. Roseman had bought Rusty a kiddie car and in Rusty's presence put it together, hoping to demonstrate that men are good for something besides doctoring. Rusty remained wary but was visually involved as he watched the action from the safety of Mrs. Roseman's lap. I felt that Rusty had indeed been able to transfer the trust he had gradually built up in me to Mrs. Roseman, who could serve both as an island of safety and a bridge to the rest of the family. I had retreated to the background in this visit and remained in another room reading a newspaper.

In conference we decided that I should begin to step out of the picture even more and have the Rosemans become more involved for longer periods of time and in different ways. The first step was for me to take Rusty to the Roseman home and arrange for Mrs. Roseman to return him to me at the agency. Each time I had taken Rusty to the Rosemans, I had told him what we were going to do that day: that we would go to the agency, then to his new mommy and daddy's house to visit the family, then back to the agency, and finally back to his foster home. Although it is difficult to know how much Rusty understood, I knew that respect for his worth and dignity as an individual was predicated on absolute honesty in our relationship, and on confidence on my part that together we could handle any feelings that were aroused in what we did together. Consequently, on the day I first left Rusty at the Roseman home I was confident that, although he experienced momentary anxiety when I told him I was going back to the agency, his confidence in me was such that he could trust Mrs. Roseman to bring him back to me.

On the next visit Rusty's experience with his new family was further expanded. Once again everyone was there, and he visited without me. In order to further facilitate my withdrawal from the situation, the Rosemans picked up Rusty at the agency. This step was important because the actual adoption procedure would take place in the agency. When the Rosemans arrived to pick up Rusty, I was sitting in the playroom with Rusty in my lap. He was beginning to be affected by his foster mother's anxiety over the impending separation and had left her with difficulty that morning. On the way to the agency he had been silent and subdued, although acutely attentive to my description and interpretation of what was happening. Once in the agency he had been more withdrawn than usual and had refused to leave my lap. After the Rosemans and I had exchanged greetings and had chatted for a few moments, Mr. Roseman said, "Well, let's go." Rusty put out his arms to Mrs. Roseman, indicating a desire to be picked up. Mr. Roseman and I exhanged suprised, relieved, and delighted glances.

Mrs. Roseman once again moved Rusty easily through the day's routine. Before he came back to the agency that morning, Rusty had eaten lunch with his new family and had dropped Eric and Debby off to play with friends. He had also discovered the joys of feeding part of his lunch to the ducks on a nearby pond. Rusty was coping beautifully, but it was a strain. As soon as he got into my car he fell asleep, and as he walked through the door of his foster home he gave a big sigh of relief.

Two days later was Adoption Day, a festive day for the whole family. The Roseman children arrived at the agency in their party clothes. Rusty arrived wearing the suit his new parents had given him on the previous visit and carrying the tiny suitcase his foster mother had bought for the occasion. It had been difficult for Rusty to leave his foster home. The foster mother's anxiety was infectious, and Rusty responded by clinging and crying. His foster sister carried him to my car because his foster mother was unable to do it. Her feelings were understandable, for her investment in him had been tremendous. Rusty cried as if his heart were breaking as we left his old home, but before we had gone two blocks his crying had stopped. His demeanor as we drove to the agency for the last time was subdued but expectant.

This time I, too, had to say good-bye. As we drove to the agency I explained what would occur that day, adding the fact that I would not be seeing him again. When we arrived at the agency, the Rosemans were already there. Rusty went easily to Mrs. Roseman, but he continued to look and gesture toward me. I think that he had understood that I would not be seeing him again. In order not to prolong the sadness of separation which I know I felt and I think he felt, I told Rusty good-bye and left him with his new family. That was the last time I saw Rusty, but six weeks later I received a note from the adoption worker who was supervising Rusty's placement. The note read:

> I want you to know I saw Rusty on Tuesday A.M. He looks great—full cheeks, flashing eyes, and a ready grin. He eats well and eats everything including meat and vegetables. Really *enjoys* meals. While I was there he raced around the house singing, dragging toys, shooting me playfully with a gun. He's getting very independent; he refuses to let Mrs. Roseman hold his hand going down the stairs and deliberately "tunes her out" when she admonishes him. He's just beginning to toilet train. He has lost his shyness with strangers and will go visiting anywhere with the Rosemans and will join in whatever play or fun is going on. Language is still proceeding slowly with a lot of "jabber" going on but family names are quite clear. The Rosemans are thoroughly delighted with him. They consider him a good-natured, affectionate, adaptable child and share our conviction in his health and good intelligence.

15

DISRUPTION: A RISK IN ADOPTION II

SALLIE R. CHURCHILL

Disruption is the termination of an adoptive placement prior to its finalization. This article discusses the worker's responsibilities in disruption to the child, the adoptive parents, and a future placement.

Adoptive placements are not always permanent. Despite the best efforts of a child, his[1] adoptive family, and his adoption worker, the process of mutual acceptance sometimes does not occur. Adoptive bonds do not emerge, and removal of a child from his adoptive home becomes necessary. The interruption of an adoptive placement before the legal finalization of the adoption process is called disruption. This article will discuss several aspects of disruption. It will conceptualize disruption as an unavoidable risk in Adoption II, and will describe specific interventions related to disruption that workers can use throughout the adoption process.

RISKS OF DISRUPTION

For a long time, the conviction that handicapped children, minority children, and older children could not be succesfully adopted prevented workers from developing adoptive placements for them. The risk of

Editors' Note: This is an original article. It relies heavily on a paper, "Further Observations on Disruptions" by Kathryn S. Donley, Executive Director, New York Spaulding for Children.

failure was too great! Thus, these children remained in institutions or in "temporary" foster care that turned, by default, into a series of foster homes or into long-term, insecure placements. While the risk of disruption in Adoption II is real, the rate of disruption is far less than had been feared. Donley[2] cited 1978 statistics regarding Adoption II programs that had existed for two to ten years. More than 85 percent of all older children and handicapped children placed were growing up in their original adoptive family. More than 90 percent of those who had experienced one disruption were successfully replaced in another family.

Unger et al.,[3] report on a study of twelve disruptions that occurred in the Michigan Spaulding for Children agency during a four-year period. Each was carefully examined to determine if there were ways to have predicted the disruption. Unger states, "The staff concluded there were no common experiences from disruption to disruption. Each seemed to have a noticeably different cause." In addition, no specific characteristic such as age or sex of the child, the age, marital status, income, number of adopted or biological children, religious affiliation of the parents, or geographic accessibility to the adoption program were identified as contributing significantly more than any other characteristic to the occurrence of disruption.

Donley[4] suggests that in a placement that threatens to disrupt one or more of the following three circumstances exists: (1) Unidentified factors exist in the family situation. That is, critical information was not recognized by the worker or family in their early efforts together. (2) The capacity or readiness of either the family or the child to make an adoptive attachment was misassessed. The ability to predict the effects of group and family dynamics is quite inadequate. People cannot be certain of how they will react in future situations, especially in situations which require complicated role changes and intense personal relationships. Therefore, individuals may not fulfill roles as they promised in good faith. (3) Unpredictable circumstances emerged and interfered with the normal progress of adoption. People cannot predict future events that may profoundly affect them and their ability to carry out family roles.

Disruption, then, is not predictable. Hence it must be viewed as a *possible* part of the total adoption process in each case. Workers must develop strategies and techniques to help families handle the prospect of disruption. Parents and children need to discuss this risk prior to placement. In addition, workers need to have methods to help families and children deal with the process of disruption itself, in those cases in which it occurs. Disruption of an adoption should not modify the goal of finding a permanent home for the child.

GROUNDWORK: DISRUPTION IS POSSIBLE

During the preplacement stage, there are two responsibilities each worker must assume that may lay groundwork for successfully working through a disruption. First, the worker must discuss the possibility of disruption with the family and the child prior to placement. This may be difficult for workers who are responding to a child's desperate need for a home and to a somewhat unsure set of prospective parents. Workers must be convinced that the discussion of disruption is more likely to reduce the likelihood that it will actually occur than to increase it.

All parties to Adoption II have conscious or unconscious concerns that this approach to developing a family may not work out. When the worker has frank discussions with the parents and the child of the possibility of disruption, she can point out that the agency will assume a nonjudgmental stance regarding problems within the family. It may be possible for prospective adoptive families to meet with parents who have dealt with disruption. This provides the applicants with additional evidence of the agency's respect for parents who have had to disrupt a placement.

The worker can explain the agency's procedures and availability for immediate help when such problems do arise. If crisis work is not provided by the adoption agency, the worker should alert the family to where such help is available in his community. Ideally such a discussion may enable the parents to seek help earlier in troubled placements as well as to be better prepared to work constructively when disruption is necessary.

Second, the worker must use preplacement opportunities to develop an early relationship with the family, characterized by open communication and shared responsibility. Open communication is based on what Clayton Hagen[5] refers to as the educative approach to selection and preparation of adoptive families.

Hagen emphasizes helping parents evaluate their own resources in parenting in relation to the demands of the hard-to-place child's special needs. The educative approach precludes a unilateral assessment of adoptive applicants by the agency. Families struggling to gain acceptance as "suitable" candidates for placement have no time or energy left to learn about the real placement problems. The educative approach places parents in the role of informed decision makers.

This horizontal decision-making is dependent upon open communication. Without it, parents are not as free to acknowledge their real fears or concerns. Open communication permits the worker and parents to anticipate, discuss, and possibly prevent or resolve problems in the placement. When a placement must disrupt, the parents have already been involved in a positive experience of self-evaluation that will serve as a basis for them to assess their role in the disruption. Open communication between the worker and the family is so key to successful Adoption II that Donley[6] suggests, that an agency plagued by unexpected disruptions would do well to examine the system which they use to find, recruit, and prepare families for placement.

ADOPTION II WORKERS' WITH THE FAMILY IN DISRUPTION PROCESS

Adoption II workers must provide support services to each family for a reasonable period following placement. The worker should know what to anticipate within a family when successful adoptive ties are developing, and be alert to clues that there are problems.

Initially, family members experience a sense of unfamiliarity and change when a child is placed in their home. The family may experience a temporary sense of calm and ususual togetherness. There is over-accommodation on the part of one or all of the family members—no problems are allowed to exist, not even the normal interactional problems. Often the child is afraid to let the family "know the real boy" for fear the family won't accept all facets of his behavior. This period is often referred to as the "honeymoon" period.

Sometimes, an adoptive child who has had traumatic interpersonal experiences reacts with an unusual degree of acting out, hostility, or verbal abuse. This reflects his fear of another rejection. He appears to test the parents and siblings by throwing his whole arsenal of negative behavior at them.

Following the initial period, whether a honeymoon or a "hell," family members begin to engage in a period of mutual accommodation. All experience some sense of discomfort because change is required of all. When the adoptive placement proceeds normally the discomfort lessens over time. However, when there are serious problems in a placement, the early sense of discomfort intensifies. This failure of the discomfort to diminish is the critical clue. Acknowledgement that a placement may be in trouble is painful to the family, child, and the Adoption II worker. However, intervention when problems are first noted may be a major deterrent to disruption.

Sometimes a family's efforts to solve problems are overwhelmed, and they demand that the child be removed. When disruption is demanded, the worker has been presented with a solution not a problem. The worker should not take irreversible actions until she understands what problems or problem the family or child are seeking to resolve through disruption. The worker must trade on her past working relationships with both the family and the child in order to get a brief agreement for the delay of precipitous actions.

The request to disrupt the adoption might be a reaction to a seemingly insignificant action—the straw that breaks the camel's back. Donley[7] points out that the situation is complicated because all involved may have a vague sense of personal responsibility for creating or for not solving the problem. Family members may have tried to overlook unpleasant reactions so that anger that has not been handled may erupt. Such outbursts are not always germane to the immediate situation. Much unravelling must occur before the components of the problem become clear enough for effective problem-solving to take place.

The use of crisis theory has been found useful to help families clarify problems, arrange them in order of priority, and to then select appropriate solutions. Often this process of clarifying and rank ordering problems and selecting solutions allows the family to function more effectively than they had prior to the blow-up. Clarifying problems often means helping the family members to alter their preceptions of problems that have become too painful to tolerate. The worker may help by providing information about child development, or by reinterpreting the needs of a specific child based on her experience with that child. Interpreting those behaviors differently may help the offended party tolerate them.

Conceptualizing the adoptive family as a system in disequilibrium is another theoretical tool which may be useful. In this frame of reference the problematic attitudes and behaviors are viewed in terms of interactions and transactions among family members. Despair, discouragement, and frustrations are symptoms of a system in serious disequilibruim.

Unilateral changes on the part of any family member will not resolve the crisis. Others must respond appropriately to a member's change efforts. Focusing on an individual alone as an "identified patient" may prove to be an impediment to resolving family crises. The worker identifies the patterns within the family and intervenes in such a way as to assist all members to return to or to establish a more comfortable, stable equilibrium.

The worker may determine that the family is in stress because there are too many demands being made upon its resources. Providing relief from these demands does not necessarily mean disrupting the placement. The worker may look to the community for respite care, including providing babysitters so parents may get away briefly or foster homes that offer short vacation placements. The worker may search in the community for other supports to relieve other demands impacting on placement, e.g., carpentry work in the house to make mobility possible for certain handicapped children who have become too heavy for a willing mother to carry.

Finally the worker may assess that the worker-family relationship or the worker-child relationship is too weak, too toxic, or too distorted for the worker to be accepted as a helpful person in direct contacts. While the worker remains the agency representative and is in control of major decisions regarding disruption, the worker may serve the family best by locating other resources which could serve in the direct help-giving roles. Examples of such resources are a family minister or physician, other adoptive parents, self-help organizations, or another worker within the adoption agency.

When the assessment is that the adoption placement must be disrupted, the worker must support the child and locate a new home for him. However, the agency has a commitment to the adoptive family, too. The family members must be helped to understand what has happened to them individually and as a family unit. The agency must be alert to the possibility that the family could be recruited as an adequate family for another child—albeit a child who would not present the same constellation of problems.

ADOPTION II WORKERS' ROLE WITH THE CHILD

There are three ways in which a child whose placement is about to be disrupted must be assisted. He must be informed of the dissolution of the placement. He must receive help in acknowledging and handling the consequences of the loss of the adoptive family, and in having to readjust in a new placement. Finally, the worker must locate a new family for the child.

Ideally, the child will still have a relationship with his placement worker because of her continuing support to him during the prefinalization period. The normal supportive interactions that the child has had with his worker may be intensified rapidly, and may provide the child with a secure base for handling the disruption.

The worker must arrange for the child to have the entire disruption process described in detail and in words that the child can understand. If the worker is to err in any direction it is better that she tell the child what he already knows rather than neglect to tell the child what he does not know. The worker and the child must repeat these discussions several times.

If the child is quite young, the use of toys, puppets, and playing out the experience may need to replace verbal discussions. It is best when these repeated interactions around disruption are phrased in different words or with different equipment in order to help guarantee that the child understands what is said. All too often the hurt child is afraid or too angry to acknowledge "not understanding" or "not being in the know" around the issues so critical to him, namely, who will be his family.

While the worker carries a responsibility to assure that such explanations are provided to the child, the worker should expend great effort at helping the parents themselves tell the child initially. Workers may need to provide parents with the appropriate words. Adults may not have dealt out-rightly or verbally with such painful experiences before. They, too, tend to use defenses to protect themselves.

The worker may need to offer parents support by being present when the parents talk to the child. In fact, the worker may have to exercise some mild control over the child's behavior should the child act out noisily or by running away to avoid hearing what the parents are trying to say. However it is done, it is necessary for the parents and the children to be helped to discuss the disruption together. By doing so, it may be possible to assure the child of continued adult interest and caring, and to reduce the overt or covert scapegoating and fault-finding.

REPLACEMENT

After the decision to disrupt the adoptive placement has been made, replacement generally should be as soon as possible. Placement should not be delayed while efforts are made to solve the emotional problems of the child. Such treatment may be more effective in the context and beginning security of a new placement. However, some children may be so upset by the disruption that it is predicatable that they would be unable to engage immediately in forming permanent adoptive ties. In such cases, immediate replacement may be contra-indicated. The difficulty the child is experiencing may be related to the trauma involved in the current crisis, or it may be complicated by the additive effect of several previous painful separations. When the worker thinks that a misassessment of the child's capacity to form family ties was the basic cause for the disruption, rather than the interactive pattern which developed within the family, a supportive and protective situation must be found in which the child can be reassessed and new plans for his permanent future be developed.

Donley[8] and Unger et al.[9] suggest the use of "bridging families" for children who are not yet ready to form permanent family relationships. Bridging families are experienced adoptive parents who provide a time-limited preparatory placement for children who must be removed from the adoptive family. These parents work with the adoption worker in preparing the child for permanent placement.

There are three requirements that a good bridging family must possess: high quality parenting skills; the capacity to offer friendships and supports to a child without demanding reciprocal responses; and a willingness to remain involved with the child when he leaves their home for a new family placement. When parents are recruited to be bridging parents, the Adoption II worker must clarify and emphasize the temporary aspect of the placement and discuss the risk of overinvolvement. However, these parents should be assured that by fulfilling a bridging role for a child their chances of being selected or rejected as permanent adoptive parents for him will not be negatively affected.

Obviously disruptions will occur at inconvenient times, when no adoptive homes are available for the displaced child. Bridging homes may be used for these children as well.

The fact that the bridging parents are adoptive parents for other children, and that they demonstrate a real and tangible commitment to adoption may be supportive to the children. It may help the displaced child continue to view himself as adoptable and help keep his hope of being adopted alive. A return to a foster home is quite likely to represent defeat and failure to the child.

SUMMARY

In this article we have noted that the risk of a disruption for Adoption II placements is real, though the rate is not as high as might have been anticipated. We have talked about the reasons why disruption may threaten, and how the workers may help the family decide on and develop a resolution to the existing conflicts. We have addressed how the worker's preparation of the parents may affect the quality of the disruption experience, and the child's and family's future adjustment.

In summary it can be said that we do not know enough about the impact of disruption on children, families, and workers. However, all too often we do not apply the knowledge now available.

NOTES

1. In this article the feminine pronoun is used in reference to adoption workers. The masculine pronoun is used in reference to the adoptive child. This word choice is for the ease of the reader and does not reflect a sexist bias on the part of the author.

2. Donley, Kathryn S. "Further Observations on Disruptions," New York Spaulding for Children. (n.d.)

3. Unger, Christopher, Dwarshuas, Gladys, and Johnson, Elizabeth, "Chaos, Madness and Unpredictability . . . Placing the Child with Ears like Uncle Harry's," Spaulding for Children, 1977.

4. Donley, Kathryn, op. cit.

5. Gregory, Graeme, "No Child is Unadoptable," an address to the general meeting, Children's Welfare Association of Victoria, Australia, October 27, 1972, p. 12 in this book.

6. Donley, Kathryn, op. cit.

7. Ibid.

8. Ibid.

9. Unger et al., op. cit.

Section IV

PROGRAM DEVELOPMENTS IN ADOPTION

Throughout this collection of articles it has been evident that placing children with special needs requires modifying existing adoption programs and creating new programs. Subsidized adoption, now available in one form or another in forty-two states, has been one major program development. Subsidy enables many families to adopt children who might otherwise remain in foster care.

ARENA (Adoption Resource Exchange of North America) has been established to serve as a national clearinghouse where licensed agencies may register any adoptable child for whom the agency cannot find a home. Families are also registered and when the information available to ARENA suggests a possible placement, referrals are sent to the agencies. Statewide and regional exchanges perform this function on a local basis.

One key program, Spaulding for Children, began as a private, specialized adoption agency in Chelsea, Michigan. It demonstrated that adoptive homes could be found for children that other agencies could not place, including children with multiple physical and mental handicaps. Spaulding staff now consult with other agencies in order to disseminate their effective and innovative approaches.

Some special programs have been established to serve the population of minority children that have been neglected or mistreated by adoption agencies for much too long. Adoption agencies are reforming their programs to more effectively recruit minority families and to more effectively involve them in the adoption process. The article by Herzog et al. in this section discusses some of the programmatic reforms needed to do this.

In some communities specialized agencies have been established to recruit minority families and place minority children. These agencies have been remarkably successful and have demonstrated techniques that work. Fischer describes one prototypical agency in his discussion of Homes for Black Children, a Detroit agency.

The three remaining articles in this section are suggestive of a range of new programs that Adoption II personnel are designing. Jones discusses a program of aggressive adoption that was established in a small county public agency. The adoption unit in that agency set a clear goal to reduce the number of children in foster care. The unit succeeded but not without altering the way the agency as a whole operated in several ways. The program had profound effects on the foster care staff, the courts, the foster families, and the prospective adoptive families. Program developments in adoption inevitably involve many actors if they are to succeed.

Gill's article reviews her agency's work with "the foster care/adoptive family." This program recruits families for children who are not legally free. The families agree to provide homes for such children with the expectation of adopting them if the legal issues are resolved. This program is an effort to spare the child painful moves from family to family.

Finally, Shireman and Watson discuss a program undertaken by the Chicago Child Care Society. The key tenets of this program were a focus on finding homes for waiting children, rather than finding children for families, and decision-making responsibility was allocated whenever possible to the adoptive applicants rather than to the worker. These two principles have been a key to successful programs finding homes for "real children."

16

SOME OPINIONS ON FINDING FAMILIES FOR BLACK CHILDREN

ELIZABETH HERZOG, CECELIA E. SUDIA, AND JANE HARWOOD

The authors consulted with one hundred people who were experienced in the field of adoptions or knowledgeable about black communities. Their aim was to gather informed opinions on ways to increase the availability of adoptive homes for black children. The article summarizes the respondents' views.

As a preliminary step in an effort to increase the availability of adoptive homes for black children, the Children's Bureau and George Washington University recently undertook an experience study—that is, a consultation with people selected because of their experience in the field of adoptions or because of their knowledge of black communities. The study was undertaken in the belief that these people could define some crucial elements that must be taken into account in planning a recruitment campaign: the incentives that might be built up; the obstacles that must be removed; and the facts or beliefs related to recruitment methods.

One hundred persons were interviewed in five large cities. They included adoptive parents, members of social agencies, and community representatives (persons in key positions in black communities). The interviewers, all black except one, were four social workers and one sociologist.

Editors' Note: Reprinted from Children *18:4 (July-August 1971), pp. 143-148.*

A full report of the findings was published by the Children's Bureau.[1] Here we merely outline some of the general patterns that emerged.

Two-thirds of the respondents were optimistic about the possibility of substantially increasing the number of adoptive homes available for black children. "The homes are there . . . agencies have not reached them." Only one respondent definitely said that it would be impossible to find enough adoptive homes to meet the need.

The respondents usually suggested that a decision for or against adopting would be the result of many interacting elements, or in some instances would really be a decision by default because little or no thought had been given to the subject.

Most respondents mentioned reasons for adoption, although the focus of the inquiry gave greater emphasis to other points. The more frequent reasons was love of children. "A child is a joy."

Although many mentioned, and others probably assumed inability to have a child of one's own as a reason for adopting, respondents by no means took for granted that only the childless should adopt.

WHY PEOPLE DO NOT ADOPT

The respondents discussed both parent-centered and agency-centered deterrents to adoption. Among the former were:

Lack of information. Although the child-placing "experts" were, expectably, far more informed that the "community representatives," the strong consensus among respondents was that: "People just don't know the magnitude of the problem and they should be told about it." A few pointed out, however, that other issues and problems have far higher priority for those who "are working on how to solve large social ills."

Parent-centered anxieties. Economic insecurity was mentioned by at least two-thirds of the respondents. Again and again they pointed out that black families have lower incomes, less job security, fewer economic reserves than white families.

> *You know how much blacks fear the loss of security . . . not knowing where the next money will be coming from, is a very important fact of life.*

Limited income, some pointed out, means limited space and inadequate housing, as well as insufficient funds to feed, clothe, and provide medical care for another member of the family.

Some respondents linked low and uncertain income with the readiness of needy black families to care for the children of equally needy relatives. Such families, they suggested, are hardly able to undertake more.

There are more unofficial adoptions in the black communities than official adoptions through agencies.

More than a third of the respondents said that sometimes a black man objects to adoption as "an affront to the male ego;" that "he feels it takes away from his manhood." A few suggested that this attitude is less frequent among younger and better educated men than among the older and less educated men, and one said it may be related as much to class as to color—since extreme pride in virility has been found in studies of other impoverished groups. A few others, however, emphatically denied that black men "have a certain thing about adoption."

Anxieties about the child. Well over a third of the respondents mentioned anxiety about the child as a possible deterrent. For the most part this centers on the idea of "bad blood." Would the child of parents either unable or unwilling to rear the child themselves inherit undesirable traits? The respondents who regarded such fears as deterrents tended not to view them as valid reasons against adoption. Several said that the "bad blood myth" is becoming less potent as people are better educated.

A very different anxiety about the child, mentioned occasionally, is a fear of losing him, psychologically or physically, after learning to love him: anxiety about having to tell the child he is adopted, or fear that the natural parent might want to reclaim him later. "You get very attached to a child and it would be awful to have the kid taken away." Such fears were, for the most part, viewed as groundless or exaggerated by the respondents.

AGENCY-CENTERED DETERRENTS

The deterrents to adoption mentioned most often and most vehemently concerned the policies and practices of child-placing agencies. Overall, the criticisms suggest that some popular misconceptions operate as strong deterrents to adoption; and some deterring practices already discarded by many agencies still survive among others. Some of the sharpest criticisms came from staff members of social agencies; while some of the most appreciative comments about agencies came from adoptive parents.

The agency's image. Half the respondents said that the public image of "the" social agency tends to discourage people from applying to adopt a child. The social agency, they said, is widely perceived as forbidding, threatening, as "screening out rather than screening in," as demanding perfection in adoptive parents, as sitting in judgment with power to give or to withhold.

Within this general image the respondents mentioned three major criticisms of agencies: (1) middle-class bias; (2) white orientation; (3) readiness to reject. One-third said child-placing agencies were perceived as seeking only well-educated applicants, with stable, above-average incomes, spacious homes, and middle-class manners and habits. Agencies were criticized almost as frequently as "racist"—less by deliberate intent than by unrecognized built-in biases: "They haven't really tried to understand the black community."

However, some respondents told of efforts by specific agencies to eliminate "white bias" and to modify the agency's image in the black community, although they thought not enough of this is being done. Some suggestions were offered to counteract such "institutional racism." A few recommended wholly black staffs and boards, since white social workers are "not used to black people."

> *I think there has to be some exploration of all-black agencies. We have to be in a position to set up our own definitions and criteria. Often this amounts to a totally different definition of family and environment.*

Comments concerning race and class bias came as often from white respondents as black, and more often from agency representatives than from adoptive parents or community representatives.

Social workers' attitudes. Closely related to the "image" of the social agency was the image painted of the social worker.

The most frequent criticisms involved general attitudes of social workers, such as "negative" or "judgmental," and again race and class bias. A number of comments, however, were neither critical or favorable, but rather stressed the qualities necessary for carrying out the social worker's role—the need for warmth, understanding, familiarity with community resources, and ability to conduct "interviews that are not interrogations," to "listen and really hear what people are saying," to "assess behavior beyond a superficial level," to put applicants at ease, and to "help them decide what kind of child they want."

Respondents who imputed racial bias or communication problems to the social workers sometimes suggested that those who deal with black adoptive applicants should themselves be black.

Because of lack of knowledge of language patterns and styles in the black community, I think that whites often completely misinterpret feelings that blacks express.

At least as many, however, saw the race of the social worker as far less important that skill, human understanding, and ability to communicate well with different kinds of people. Class bias was mentioned somewhat less often than "racism," and occasionally was imputed to black as well as white social workers. Social workers, it was said "fail to recognize the strengths in poor families." Several respondents suggested that agencies provide inservice training to help staff members overcome problems of attitude and communication.

Specific agency deterrents. The length of time and the redtape involved in completing the adoption process were frequently mentioned as deterrents. Many respondents suggested that the process could be streamlined, but said that even now the redtape is probably not as excessive as is generally believed.

The redtape people expect really turns them off. You hear hearsay, such as there's a lot of redtape; you have to be the parents of the year in order to get a child. . . .(but) I went through less for this adoption than for a lot of other things.

Feelings were mixed, however, about efforts some adoption agencies are making to reduce the waiting period for black applicants, some interpreting this as evidence of a double standard for whites and blacks.

The agency seemed not to be able to stick to a standard where a black child was involved. I know it's hard to place black children, but should just any *home be accepted?*

Agencies' criteria for adoptive parenthood were regarded as deterrents by a substantial minority of the respondents. They recommended less emphasis on externals, such as income and housing. What matters most, they said or implied, is that adoptive parents should love children and be able to give them firm guidance.

The agency makes you feel like you got to move up and dress fine rather than just being able to love and to help a child be well adjusted and allow the child to grow.

Many respondents suggested helping potential adoptive parents with financial supplements, if necessary. On the whole, however, those who mentioned "external" requirements leaned to the opinion that adoptive parents should be able to support their families without assistance. Several respondents gave evidence that agency requirements on income are less stringent than supposed.

A requirement that an adoptive mother should stop working was viewed as a serious deterrent for many black families in the few places that still have such a rule.

Among specific deterrents mentioned as existing in many, though not all, agencies were inconvenient location and hours, rigidity in rules and practices, agency fees, and lawyers' fees.

The adoption study. The intensiveness of the study that precedes acceptance of an applicant was reported as a deterrent by over half of the respondents. Adoptive parents tended to be less critical than agency respondents but more critical than community representatives. The criticism centered on "nosey" and "humiliating" psychological probing, regarded as excessive and incompatible with the lifestyle of many potential adoptive parents.

> *Asking a person how they feel about something is very middle class. Many people aren't used to discussing their feelings.*

While a few defended the necessity to "screen applicants carefully so 'undesirables' will not be accepted," most respondents stressed a need to reduce psychological study to a minimum.

Efforts to match the characteristics of a child to those of the adoptive parents were referred to by less than a third of the respondents—sometimes as deterrents, sometimes as incentive to adoption. No consensus emerged about whether agencies should or should not try to match, nor about how much or how effectively they try, but there was evidence that both agencies and applicants are not less insistent about matching than they once were. A few said growing recognition that "black is beautiful" has reduced black applicants' desire for a light child.

Inquiry into the existence and basis of infertility in the adoptive applicants was decried as arousing anxiety and distaste in prospective adoptive applicants, especially men. A sure way to lose an applicant, it was said, is to inquire about causes of childlessness during the initial telephone conversation.

From the initial application to completion, adopting a child was usually seen as a tense and anxious process. About one-fourth of the respondents said the agency could allay the anxiety by explaining the procedures to be followed and the reasons for them, providing feedback where appropriate, and maintaining contact with the applicants.

ENLARGING THE TARGET GROUP

Again and again the respondents stressed the need for agencies to reach for adoptive parents beyond the traditional target group—white middle or upper income childless couples between the ages of twenty-five and forty. They were asked about a number of possibilities: single or widowed persons; couples with a different racial background than the child's; older couples; couples whose income must be subsidized to make the adoption possible; and the child's foster parents. A recurrent comment was that the special type of placement under consideration, whatever its disadvantages, is better than letting the child grow up in unstable foster care or in an institution.

One parent adoptions. More than two-thirds of the respondents expressed outright approval of single-parent adoptions, and very few expressed outright disapproval. "One parent is better than none," they often said. Approval was repeatedly linked, however, with stipulations that the age and sex of the child must be appropriate—usually defined as past infancy and of the same sex as the adopting parent—and that the motivation and personal makeup of the applicants must be carefully studied.

For the most part, a single parent adoption was viewed as adoption by a woman. The most frequency qualifications of approval related to the need for the adoptive mother to be mature, responsible, emotionally stable, economically adequate, and able to provide male models and companions for the child. The relatively few who expressed misgivings about such adoptions warned against the possible motivations of one-parent applicants—they may be impelled by their own need rather than by interest in and ability to care for a child. Some respondents approved such adoptions as a second choice, acceptable only if a two-parent home is unavailable, but others saw them as "a desirable alternative."

Only a few respondents included unattached men in their consideration of single-parent homes but among those, approval—usually qualified—was far more frequenct than disapproval. The chief objection was that a man would find it more difficult than a woman to be both mother and father to a child.

Cross-racial adoptions. No subject evoked stronger expressions of feeling among the respondents than "transracial" adoptions. Approval was somewhat more frequent than either disapproval or no definite judgment, but disapproval was expressed with more intensity.

Those who spoke from direct experience or observation came out two to one in favor of cross-racial adoptions. Those who based their views on hearsay or on principle—chiefly the community respresentatives—were a little more often opposed than in favor. Black respondents divided evenly for and against such placements, while whites were a little more often in favor than opposed.

The main reasons for favoring transracial adoptions were belief that there are not enough black adoptive homes available to meet the need, that such adoptions are better than none for children in need of families, and that white couples who want to adopt black children are likely to have good potential for parenthood.

> *Most people thinking about adopting transracially know they'll have problems, but they have the strength to come to grips with them.*

Leading all reasons for opposition was the problem of identity, mentioned by one-third of all the respondents, including some who give mixed or qualified opinions.

> *White families could never provide a black experience for a black child. They could never adequately help a child with his black identity and pride in his heritage.*

Even if the immediate family experienced no problems, it was argued, the child might suffer from negative attitudes of relatives, neighbors, schoolchildren, teachers, and the general community. "He will never feel really accepted."

A scornful fraction of the respondents raised questions about the "real" motivation of white parents who adopt a black child. Such adoptive parents, they suggested, are impelled either by social guilt or by an image of themselves as model liberals.

> *When you talk with them, they say everything is happy, or fine and lovely, but they don't know what the child is thinking and they don't know what kind of problems he has because they are too busy taking care of their own needs.*

Two respondents mentioned that two black social workers' organizations have taken a stand against cross-racial adoptions.

Strong opposition was occasionally coupled with the charge that, instead of really trying to find black adoptive homes, the agencies are "going all out to find white homes for them."

> *Transracial adoption should be the last and final resort. No matter how hard they might seem to have tried, no agency has made a concerted effort to reach black people who could adopt all these available children.*

Respondents with certain views said that a transracial adoption should be considered only if no other alternative exists except an institution; that it is still too early to know how black children will fare after ten years as part of a white family; and that because the outcome will depend on the individuals involved, such adoptions must rest on careful preplacement evaluation not only of the adoptive applicants, but also of their neighborhood, the climate of their community, and the attitudes of their relatives.

Subsidized adoption. Nearly three-fourths of the respondents expressed some opinion about subsidized adoptions, their views running ten to one in favor, very few against, and a few mixed.

The chief reasons given for approval were that subsidy would make the homes available for many people who would make good parents but cannot afford to adopt—foster parents who have grown attached to the children in their care, young couples who would need only short-term subsidies until their incomes become adequate to provide for a child's needs, and perhaps even public assistance recipients.

However, a few agency people reported that in some places where adoption subsidy is legally authorized, "agency staffs aren't accepting the idea." "People just aren't being referred."

There were a few suggestions for a Federal program of adoption subsidy.

> *We subsidize everything including the military and the large farmowner so why should we not subsidize adoption—a human commodity?"*

The few respondents who disapproved or had mixed opinions about subsidized adoption expressed concern about the adoptive parents' motives. "One would have to be sure it was for love of the child rather than for love of the money."

Foster-parent adoptions. Less than one-third of the respondents mentioned adoption by foster parents. Those who did generally approved, but their approval was often qualified by reference to the need for individualized evaluation. No support was given to the rule some States have against allowing foster parents to adopt a child already in their care.

There were two main reasons for approval: (1) That adoption by his foster parents would bring the child a "real home of his own" and remove the threat of further placements; (2) that the foster parents' desire to adopt the child must mean that they have learned to love him. A few respondents suggested foster care as a kind of trial adoption. Qualifications of approval usually concerned differences in criteria for selecting foster and adoptive parents.

Older parents. Almost two-thirds of the respondents expressed no clear-cut opinion in regard to adoption by older persons, but among the opinions expressed more than five out of six were favorable.

> *Rather than a blanket policy (on age), each individual should be evaluted. There are people in their 60's much better able to be parents. . . .I was raised by my grandparents.*

Most of those who approved, however, pointed out that by "older" they did not mean "really old," but merely older than the age agencies usually consider appropriate. Some said "not over 50," the age at which many people first become grandparents.

Many respondents pointed to the importance of considering the adoptive parents' health, energy and the ability to "think young," and of their having available close, interested relatives to serve as an extended family for the child.

RECRUITING ADOPTIVE PARENTS

Most of the respondents offered a good deal of advice on how to recruit more adoptive applicants, some from direct experience.

The mass media. Use of the mass media—television, radio, newspapers, magazines—was far the most frequent, and often the only, method of recruitment mentioned. Two main functions were emphasized: (1) moving people to apply for an adoptive child; and (2) spreading information relating to the magnitude and the urgency of the need, the dispelling of "myths" about adoptive families and adoptive children, and the dispelling of misconceptions about agency policies and practices with regard to adoption. Television was the preferred medium.

However, a small proportion of the respondents, expressed the opinion that the effort and expense of such a campaign is out of proportion to the number of placements actually achieved. They pointed out that when shortage of staff and funds prevent a quick followup of the greatly increased number of inquiries, applicants tend to drop out.

> *In the recruitment campaign we got over 100 inquiries and completed about five home studies.*

Several respondents suggested that for mass media appeals to be most useful they must be carried out in conjunction with more direct person-to-person contacts.

Personal contact. About one-fourth of all the respondents emphasized the value of a personal approach in some form. Some favored using a full-time recruiter, preferably black. Others suggested involving paraprofessionals from a poverty agency.

> There are many potential adopters being missed in low-income groups. Agencies need to get out and talk to the black people. The emphasis must be on reaching the people where they are.

Adoptive parents. Many respondents, including some adoptive parents, suggested the use of adoptive parents as recruiters. Some cited instances in which the example of happy adoptive families has stimulated friends and acquaintances to seek adoptive children. Others recommended group meetings in which adoptive parents tell about their own rewarding experiences. A community representative suggested having new applicants meet with an adoptive parent after the first interview "to relieve the tensions."

Almost as many opposed as approved attempts to involve adoptive parents in recruitment efforts, usually because they found, or believed, that this is regarded as an invasion of privacy.

Community approaches. Churches and other local organizations and community groups were frequently mentioned as channels for recruitment efforts. Respondents with direct experience were more pessimistic than others about recruitment through churches. Those who endorsed such efforts said that clergymen could help to dispel some deterring myths. The skeptics said that church appeals have not produced results because (1) they have been "one-shot" events rather than sustained programs; (2) they have been directed toward middle-class congregations; (3) they have relied on posters or brochures rather than person-to-person contacts.

Opinions were divided about the usefulness of setting up local committees to stimulate recruitment efforts—the division apparently being based on differences in experience. Among local groups cited as helpful were fraternal organizations, PTA's, industrial firms, professional associations and unions.

Coordination and collaboration. A recurrent theme in the recruitment recommendations, especially of those with direct experience, was the need for planned, sustained, coordinated methods employed by cooperating agencies, groups, and individuals. The most enthusiastic success stories tended also to involve sustained, coordinated efforts *within* agencies; modification of deterring practices; and preparation to cope with increased applications.

A major block to effective coordination, some experienced social workers said, is lack of trust between agencies and the unwillingness of some to accept work done by another agency. They saw a need for a "true community of agencies": on the local, State, and national levels.

THE MESSAGE

Thus, the major message delivered by these respondents was a plea for more "integration" in a special sense: through broadening the definition of potential adoptive parents to include groups and individuals formerly left out of consideration; and through combining various methods of recruitment in a planned, sustained, and truly coordinated effort.

NOTES

1. Herzog, Elizabeth, Sudia, Cecelia E., Harwood, Jane. Families for Black Children: The Search for Adoptive Parents. U.S. Department of Health, Education and Welfare, Office of Child Development, Children's Bureau, 1971.

17

HOMES FOR BLACK CHILDREN

CLARENCE D. FISCHER

A special Detroit agency demonstrates that a focus on recuiting black families and placing black children bears results. The successful approaches of this agency are outlined. In the end, the author asserts that more money must be allocated and more black professional staff hired to carry out this work.

In recent years many agencies across the country have developed imaginative and creative programs for finding permanent adoptive homes for children who have been called "hard to place." Hundreds of children, once considered unadoptable, are now gaining the parents they need and deserve. Arbitrary and artifical eligibility requirements are waived by most agencies to enable them to look at all prospective applicants for what is really imporant, the ability to give the love and security that will allow the child to grow to mature adulthood.

Even though this changing pattern has existed in Michigan and in the metropolitan Detroit area, one group has still been denied adoption in large numbers. This group consists of black and black-Caucasian children. In 1967 all of the agencies reporting to United Community Services of Metropolitan Detroit, a community planning agency, placed ninety-three black children for adoption. This was less than 3 percent of the illegitimate births for such children. In the same year these agencies placed 1,331 white children—40 percent of the illegitimate births.

Although this illustrated an obvious discrepancy in availability of a needed service, many still insisted that there was no problem. Following are a few of the attitudes frequently expressed: "After all, the black culture does not permit the giving away of children." "Everyone knows the unwed mother and her illegitimate child are easily assimilated into the family in the black community." "The statistics on unrelated adoptions do not take into account the high number of related adoptions among black people. Those figures show that large numbers of black children are being adopted."

United Community Services established an Illegitimacy Study Committee, which examined this question in depth during 1968. The attitudes cited were shown to be either myths or a way for the community to absolve itself of guilt for its failure to provide the needed services. The study proved that black families had little or no choice on adoptions.

Incomplete statistics indicated there were more than 300 black children in foster care in the Detroit area who were available for adoption. Further, it appeared there were several hundred additional black children in foster care who were temporary public wards, where parental rights had not been severed because permanent adoptive homes were not available. Many of these children had waited from five to ten years for adoption.

It was not difficult to find other evidence of need for expanding adoption services for black children. Every boarding home spot in the community available to black children was almost continuously filled. The private maternity homes, a program to provide medical care for indigent mothers, and a continuing-education program for pregnant teenagers in the inner city all had the same problem. The committee was often unable to find an agency, public or private, that could assume responsibility for providing boarding care and adoption services for a black infant even when the mother was begging for service. Dozens of black unwed mothers were denied service of any kind, and were forced to take babies home even though they knew it was impossible to provide adequately for them.

The Illegitimacy Study Committee proposed that a special adoption program be established to recruit adoptive applicants for black children, prepare families for adoption, and arrange placements. The program was expected to be innovative and experimental. It was not to replace other agencies' services, but to supplement them. It was to be completely nonsectarian, with approved families being made available for children waiting in any community agency, public or private. It was decided that the program should be administered by an existing agency, rather than creating a new agency. It was believed that such an approach would be more economical and could be organized, staffed, and begin functioning more quickly.

The staff of United Community Services, with the help of the Illegitimacy Study Committee, developed a program proposal, applied to the United Foundation of Metropolitan Detroit, and received a special grant of $99,500 from the Urban Crisis Fund of United Foundation, in March 1969. The grant was to provide a program director and five social workers and pay for office space, equipment, transportation, and secretarial services. United Community Services selected the Lutheran Children's Friend Society to administer the program. The goal was set for 100 placements in the first full year of operation.

GOAL SURPASSED

In June 1969, the director, one caseworker, and a secretary began to work. The program moved into its own quarters in July and the name Homes for Black Children was adopted. September 1, 1969, was set as the beginning of the first full year of operation, although only one child had been placed and the program was not fully staffed.

On May 27, 1970, the 100th placement was arranged by Homes for Black Children—more than three months prior to the target date and less than a year from the time the first staff member joined the program. By August 31, the end of the first year, 135 black children had found permanent homes. Following are some reflections on why the program succeeded.

The staff consists of a program director, five social workers, and two secretaries. Two caseworkers are white; the rest of the staff is black. The publicity is built around a black program director, to encourage a positive response from the black community. Having a black receptionist to answer the phone and welcome families into the office also seems to have a major impact. There appears to be no problem because some staff members are white. There has been no recruitment of applicants beyond utilizing excellent cooperation offered by the mass media. Actually, it was necessary to keep publicity at a low key to avoid becoming overwhelmed with applicants. We believe we could recruit enough black families in the Detroit area to keep twenty social workers busy.

Only one of the 135 placements has been with a white family. Since there were more applicants than could be utilized, we started referring all white families to other agencies. It was also possible to refer most black Catholic families to Catholic social services. This referral of applicants corresponded with a desire to assist all agencies in expanding services for black children. In 1969, 253 black children were placed for adoption by the Detroit area agencies, illustrating that Homes for Black Children was simply part of the total community thrust.

Recruitment aimed at eliciting sympathy is completely ineffectual in the black community. Some adoption publicity is insulting and derogatory to the black community, particularly that which implies that black families are not interested in children and white families are. We try to build newspaper articles and news releases around the concept that black families have always adopted at a much higher rate than white families, although the arrangements have usually been informal. Recruiting based on demonstrated concern and love for children by the black community obtains the best results, while expressing a simple truth.

The great need in the black community is education. The most important point to communicate is that not all institutions of society and not all social agencies must be distrusted. It is obvious that most agencies are designed to serve white families and are controlled by whites. Agencies designed to serve whites do not serve blacks effectively. Wrong judgments are often made about black families because they do not respond the same way to the agency adoption process as white families.

This stresses the importance of the name of the program—Homes for Black Children. Black families come to Homes for Black Children with an expectation that they will be treated with consideration. Such positive expectations greatly assist them in utilizing the services or accepting the process. With good reason, black families have rarely been able to approach other community facilities with positive expectations. It is essential to select an agency name which conveys its identity.

EXPERIMENTS IN APPROACH

We are experimenting with different processes, and have reached several definite conclusions. A great deal of time is needed to handle the initial inquiry. Since most black families are suspicious of agencies and do not expect fair treatment, the agency must reach out. It is inappropriate to begin any process with black families by mailing out applications and expecting them to return them.

The approach that seems to work the best is to assign an individual worker as quickly as possible. An appointment is offered at the place the family prefers, either in the office, or at their home. Most families prefer the home. Usually additional interviews can be easily and comfortably arranged in the office. Since the preplacement work of most agencies includes one home call, no time would be wasted in making this the first interview.

Another experimental process includes two meetings for a group of couples, and then assignment to individual workers. This is more effective in preparing couples to become adoptive parents, if they are willing and able to participate. We also plan to experiment with handling all of the preplacement work in groups.

Although couples are invited to participate in groups by letter, a followup telephone call is made to explore their interests. We also followup by phone those couples who agree to attend, but do not show up for the meeting. With black couples, it is inappropriate to assume lack of motivation for adoption if they do not respond as we have always expected white couples to respond. Regardless of the process, application blanks should be given in person, if they are used, and should even be filled out by the worker unless the couples are comfortable in completing them. Many black families have a limited educational background, and others have often been rejected in other areas, such as employment, on the basis of completed application blanks, so there is fear and resistance.

In most metropolitan areas, there has been a good response from black families to mass media publicity. When there is not a corresponding rapid increase in black placements, it may be assumed that the process does not relate itself appropriately to the needs and fears of black families. Another obstacle may be the approach in dealing with adoptive applicants, regardless of the process used.

Although an investigative approach can be used with white applicants for white infants with little or no risk of running out of families, it is still destructive of positive adoption services. The investigative approach simply will not work at all with black families. Unless the agency is really committed to helping people to sort through their fears and anxieties with a nonjudgmental approach, and willing to devote time to this, many good potential families are lost. When this happens, one can only conclude the agency is basically not interested in placing black children for adoption. Even when terms such as "study" and "evaluation" are used (they are slightly more acceptable than "investigation") the goal of most workers is to collect data to make a decision to accept or reject. This is normally a one-way and not a two-way process. If the approach usually used in adoption were used in family counseling, no family's adjustment would ever be improved.

HIGH-LEVEL SERVICE NEEDED

When a special adoption program is set up to place children waiting in a variety of community agencies, it is essential to provide a high level of service. By this we do not mean a high level of cancellations. Every effort must be made to help families to become adoptive parents. There is no need to cut corners with black families by having only brief, superficial contacts. They will stay in a process that is designed for them. Placements were arranged in cooperations with thirteen different agencies, in the first year.

I believe agencies can achieve a marked increase of placements with black families by utilizing the techniques of the Homes for Black Children project. However, a program with a separate identity is essentialy for substantial changes. This does not necessarily mean a separate agency; in most cases several years would be lost in setting up a separate agency, costs would be higher, and recruitment of appropriate staff might be complicated. But the separate identity must be real, including office space, stationery and publicity materials.

A final point is that the greatest need in this area is action. Money must be allocated and competent black staff employed. If this is done and staff are given the right and responsibility to design the process, the job can be easy. Many communities have discussed this problem and planned solutions for years. More discussion is not the need; it may simply be the excuse for continuing to deny desperately needed homes to black children. It takes staff and money to place white children with white parents. It is safe to conclude that the same is true for placing black children with black parents, but the money has not be allocated.

18

AGGRESSIVE ADOPTION: A PROGRAM'S EFFECT ON A CHILD WELFARE AGENCY

MARTHA L. JONES

An adoption program aggressively carried out, not only achieved its goal of reducing the number of children in long-term foster care, but had beneficial effects on other services by the agency.

A separate adoption unit was established in the Cumberland County Children's Services (Carlisle, Pennsylvania) in June 1972. Until then few adoptions had been handled by the agency, and those had been assigned to the ongoing caseworker. The goal of the new unit was to reduce the number of children in long-term foster care by making adoptive plans for as many as possible. Initially the adoption unit worked with children who had been in long-term foster care—two years or more—but the agency soon moved into prevention of such care, with adoption as the alternative.

Much has been written about the detrimental effect of long-term foster care on children (Mass and Engler, 1959), and the advisability of making permanent plans as early as possible (Goldstein et al., 1973). The agency had not failed to recognize the needs of children for permanence. It supported the idea of swift permanent plans, but structurally was unable to carry this out. The establishment of a separate, aggressive adoption unit has been effective in meeting this problem. In the four years that the unit has been functioning, the number of children in foster care has been reduced by 33 percent, and the number of children in care from two to five years has been reduced to 53 percent. The long-range projection is for continued reductions, since few are now remaining in care for more than two years. Indirect results have included a change in staffing patterns that allows for more services to children in their own homes, and a reduction in staff turnover in the agency's foster unit.

ESTABLISHMENT OF A UNIT

The first step was to study state and federal adoption laws, with guidance from the agency's attorney as to evidence needed to terminate parental rights. As court experience was gained, the unit became more aware of what was required to prove a case in court. For example, testimony from case records can be ruled hearsay, and therefore inadmissable, unless it is given by the worker who dictated the entry. To deal with this the unit called back caseworkers who had been away for many years. The practice of recording crucial information in letter form, which is admissible, has also been established.

Following this research, the records of all children who had been in foster care for six months or more were reviewed to determine who might be candidates for adoption. Three questions were considered:

(1) Has the agency made every possible effort to rehabilitate the family?
(2) Has the family still failed to take steps to provide a home for the child?
(3) If the answers to both questions are yes, can both points be proved in court?

Once children who were candidates for adoption had been identified, the cases were taken to court. The unit started with those where there was little doubt about the lack of interest by the natural parents, and worked through the list to cases that might require rulings by higher courts.

It quickly became apparent how poor the case records were for court use. The Pennsylvania adoption law (1970) stipulates that parental rights can be terminated involuntarily for failure of parents to perform parental duties. The courts further require that the agency establish that the parents were given every opportunity to make a plan for the child, received all possible assistance from within the agency to do so, and were not encouraged to absent themselves from the scene.

The old case records did not indicate clearly what had been said to parents about making a plan. This made it difficult to establish that they had failed to meet their obligations. Furthermore there was little recorded evidence of agency efforts to rehabilitate families or to locate missing parents. These shortcomings in the records led to involvement of the total staff in the potential adoption plans.

In addition to the question of parental activity in relation to the children, the agency also faced the issue of adoptive family recruitment. For many years adoption had been considered primarily for infants and preschoolers, and the agency was not initially sure adoptive families could be found for the school-age children with behavioral problems who were now adoptable. It also faced the question of foster family adoption of their foster children. The results of the agency's efforts are encouraging: of the 116 children placed for adoption in the last five years, only two have not been legally adopted.

INVOLVEMENT OF THE TOTAL AGENCY

During the first six months of the program, adoption was arranged for twenty waiting children. The next move was to involve the entire staff in the effort to make permanent plans for children. A policy affecting all units in the agency was established.

It was decided that beginning in January 1973 all children in foster care six months or more would be considered for adoption. The aggressiveness of the adoption unit forced foster and protective service workers to formulate clear goals with their clients. Basically this meant the following:

(1) At the time of placement specific goal plans (Houts and Scott, n.d.) are set up with families, outlining in detail what is to be done by the agency and by the family in order to return the children to their home.
(2) A time limit of six months is written into the goal plan, with a statement that after that time the agency will pursue an adoption plan.
(3) All progress or lack of it on the goal plan is documented by letter for possible court use.

The initial objective was more and better documentation of parents' performance of their responsibilities to their children. This was primarily for use in adoption cases. The adoption unit is now able to document in court all efforts by the agency to help parents assume responsibility, all failed appointments, visits and so forth. When a petition is filed for termination of parential rights, it makes clear to parents and court that a workable plan was agreed upon, that the agency fulfilled its part of the contract, and that the parents failed to do so.

Another purpose of the adoption unit is to make sure that good permanent plans were made for children—not just to use adoption as a goal for children. The agency policy was designed to affect all areas of the child welfare program and it does. For example, in the past many families were not involved in goal planning for the return of their children. There was an implicit understanding between family and agency that the parents were not capable of rearing their children, and that the agency would rear them in foster care. Vague goals were set for parents, such as getting a better apartment, demonstrating stability or maintaining an adequate income. When families achieved these vague goals, the agency came up with a new set of goals.

The new policy calls for clear behavioral goals mutually agreeable to parent and agency. Thus, a family needs a two-bedroom apartment with running water and kitchen facilities rather than a "better apartment." Casework with the family is goal-directed, with the worker helping to break down the long-term objective into short-term, achievable goals. A family might be expected in a two-week period to contact three landlords and look at one apartment that might meet their needs. Realistic time limits are set, with a period of more than six months considered unrealistic. As a result, more of those children placed in temporary foster care are being returned to their parents.

EFFECTS ON FOSTER FAMILIES

In addition to improved communication between agency workers and natural families, there has been clearer understanding among workers, natural families and foster families. Prior to the new policy, foster families were never sure how long a placement would last. If ultimate goals had been unclear to natural families, they were even more vague to foster families. Since the agency goal now is a permanent plan as soon as possible, foster families must be part of the team working on that plan. When natural parents consistently fail to show up for visits, the foster families know that they have to participate in preparing the child for adoption. Equally important, when parents make progress toward their goals, foster families take pride in their part of the realization of these goals.

Under the new policy, the agency has experienced less turnover of foster parents, fewer foster placements per child, and greater cooperation between foster parents and agency workers. These improvements are attributed to the increased clarity of agency expectations of foster parents and the agency's demonstrated ability to live up to promises about the future of the children.

Because of the earlier reluctance of the agency to take action to ensure permanence and security for children, many foster families felt that it was up to them to protect the children. This resulted in the sabotaging of some plans for the return of children to their natural families. Traces of this attitude remain, but more foster families are now actively involved in the rehabilitation of natural families. Generally foster families are advocates of the rights of children, and when they become convinced that a natural parent will not take responsibility for the child, they support adoption as a second choice.

SELECTION OF ADOPTIVE FAMILIES

When adoption is considered for many formerly "unadoptable" children, it is necessary to take a new look at adoption resources. Since security and permanence for the child are primary goals, foster families have been the primary resource for children in long-term care. When such a child is considered for adoption, the plan is discussed with the foster family, and they are generally the first choice for the child's permanent home. When foster families choose to adopt, the move is generally smooth and comfortable for all concerned.

We had thought that families who had parented a child for more than two years would want to adopt that child, but many foster families chose not to adopt children who had been in their homes for three to seven years—and occasionally longer. The relationship had been seen as temporary by child and family alike, probably as a protection from the hurt of an intimate relationship. Even very young children seem aware that a foster home is not the same as "home." The children who were moved from their long-term foster home to an adoptive home made rapid adjustments and often made great improvements in social, emotional, and educational skills. Some chose to change their first name as well as their last, in a symbolic rebirth. Several who were adopted by their foster families showed similar, though less dramatic, signs of relaxing, trusting, and belonging.

The search for families for those adoptable children led to some conclusions about the criteria to be used in the selection. Many of the most effective adoptive families have children of their own, adopting more out of their knowledge that they parent well than because they need another child. This is not to say that couples with children are always more effective adoptive families than childless couples, but the couples most desperate for children are often looking for a child to meet their needs. Couples who have more options, who can live happily with or without children, are generally more able to accept adoptable children, complete with a past and some problems.

EFFECT OF PROGRAM ON TOTAL AGENCY

The effect of this aggressive adoption program on the foster caseload is documented in statistics collected since its inception. In the first two years the sum total of foster care was reduced from 27 percent of the total agency caseload to 18 percent. This reduction has been maintained for more than three years. The financial savings are obvious. Another benefit has been the change in agency staffing patterns because of the adoption program.

The number of children in care for less than one year has remained constant since 1970. There have been encouraging changes in other categories. On December 31, 1971, there were 47 children who had been in care from two to five years. This number was reduced to 22 by December 31, 1975, a 53 percent decrease. In addition, there was a reduction from 32 to 19 children in care 5 to 7 years, and from 70 to 51 in care 7 or more years. It is expected that in the next few years these categories will continue to drop. If an adequate adoption subsidy were available to foster families, a further dramatic drop in the number of children in long-term care could be expected.

Obviously, the agency's foster care caseloads have been reduced substantially. Since the number of children receiving service has remained relatively constant, this has allowed for a shift in manpower. The number of foster care caseworkers in the agency has been reduced, and services to children in their own homes have been increased. The larger protective service staff continues to see most of the families served. An increase in day care services and increased manpower in the protective unit have enabled these services to be more effective in helping children in their own homes.

The foster care workers retained in that role have shown a much lower rate of turnover than previously. This is attributed to the greater movement within their caseloads. The agency finds that the worker's greatest effort with families occurs in the first six months of the case. Since children generally are not with the agency much longer than that, they receive maximum services from their caseworkers.

Our agency is a relatively small public agency. Although it was interested in expanding protective and day care services for many years, it did not have the resources to carry out new, progressive programs. The relief of having made permanent plans for many children who would have been the long-term responsibility of the community has made the key difference for the agency. The goal of making secure permanent plans for children in the agency's care was the only one in mind when the adoption unit was established. The success of the program has provided added benefits: a structure for more effective casework with families in the form of goal plans, and a redistribution of staff allowing more time and energy for intensive work with needy families.

REFERENCES

Goldstein, Joseph, Freud, Anna and Solnit, Albert J. (1973) *Beyond the Best Interests of the Child,* New York: Free Press.

Houts, Peter, and Scott, Robert. "Goal Planning in Mental Health Rehabilitation." Department of Behavioral Science, Penn State University, Milton S. Hershey Medical Center, Hershey, PA 17033. Training material developed by contract from NIMH, HEW Washington, D.C.

Maas, Henry S., and Engler, Richard E. (1959) *Children in Need of Parents.* New York: Columbia University Press.

Pennsylvania Adoption Act of 1970, PL 620 (1 P.S. 101 et. seq.).

19

THE FOSTER CARE/ADOPTIVE FAMILY: ADOPTION FOR CHILDREN NOT LEGALLY FREE

MARGARET GILL

A program has been developed in which children not legally free for adoption are placed with foster families who are committed to adoption, while accepting the risk that the children may not become legally free. The program is designed to eliminate the damage of interim foster placements. It has proved effective, though presenting some special problems.

Child welfare workers have traditionally operated on the premise that a child not legally free for adoption could be placed only in a temporary foster home. This often resulted in a child's experiencing several foster homes before legal resolution of the situation permitted permanent placement. At Lutheran Child and Family services, a program has been developed in which a family serves as foster parents for a child not legally free for adoption at the time of placement, with the expectation of becoming the child's adoptive parents if legal issues are resolved. The intention of the placement is adoption, obviously different from that of traditional foster care.

The basic reason for developing this program was to spare a child interim moves. However, many disadvantages have become apparent since the program began in the summer of 1973. First, since the intention is adoption, though this cannot be guaranteed, the parents make a

Editors' Note: Copyright 1975 by Child Welfare League of America. Reprinted with permission from Child Welfare *LIV: 10 (1975), pp. 712-720.*

commitment to the child far beyond that typical of traditional foster care. Second, this type of placement appears to strengthen the agency's legal position in several ways. Juvenile court cases have not been unnecessarily delayed, since there is a family interested in the final outcome. The Juvenile Court judge seems more confident in terminating parental rights when he knows that the family caring for the child also wishes to adopt him. Further, since the agency's private lawyers are involved in the cases, many of which concern State Department children, early decision-making has been forced. The attorneys are active, committed, and aware of the procedures followed by the state's attorney. This has meant that common court mistakes have been avoided. Summons are now sent out, requests for publications are acted on, and so forth. This has made fewer court continuances necessary; hence the legal situation is resolved much sooner, and the child is no longer in legal limbo, with the resulting emotional problems.

An example of how the agency's legal case could have been strengthened by having a Foster Care/Adoptive family occurred in a situation of married parents who had voluntarily relinquished their eighteen-month-old child. The biological grandparents would not accept this decision, and threatened to sue the agency. There were no families available who had been prepared to handle such a legal risk, so the child was moved into regular foster care. This upset the natural parents, and they decided not to stand firm against their parents. Had a Foster Care/Adoptive family been prepared and waiting, the case might have ended differently.

A third advantage of the program is that it not only helps the child, but helps the biological parents in making a decision to relinquish. Particularly in situations where they have parented a child for months or years, the parents are better able to accept the permanency of the decision if they are given some time before signing final relinquishments. Typically, children are moved from their biological family to foster care to an adoptive family. Through a Foster Care/Adoptive family, the biological parents can have the time they need emotionally to surrender the child while knowing the child does not have to experience an interim family.

INTERPRETATON AT INTAKE

At intake, the agency informs applicants of the various needs of children waiting for permanent families. The legal need is considered as legitimate as any other need, such as age and handicap. The majority of Foster Care/Adoptive families come to the agency through adoption intake rather than foster care intake. These prospective adoptive families have expanded their flexibility to include legal risks. This creates a different type of placement from one in which foster parents decide to adopt the child they are parenting—a situation prevalent in foster care for many years. The difference involves the initial intent and commitment to the child.

The applicant family must be mature, realistic and extremely flexible. This program is not a backdoor to the placement of healthy infants or toddlers. At the start of the program, many families were settling unrealistically for Foster Care/Adoption as a quick path to adoption. The agency had to help such families appraise realistically their capacity to handle the risk involved. On the other hand, families were not limited to this program.

PREPARATION PROCESS

Obviously, such complicated placements require careful preparation of the new parents. It is vital that the worker and family engage in a casework relationship that promotes mutual trust and realistic decision-making. Crucial to this are the philosophy and principles of practice upon which the agency's approach to adoption is based. For many years Lutheran Child and Family Services has operated through a worker-family partnership in which preparation for adoption holds central focus. This approach is a way of integrating adoption practice with social work's basic principles: client's right to self-determination; upholding the dignity of the individual; worker nonjudgmentalism. It eliminates the need for "approving" or "rejecting" families and substitutes a helping process. This approach is of special significance in Foster Care/Adoption practice.

There are some unique aspects to Foster Care/Adoption preparation. One major point: the family must be clear about risk. Some families may fantasy that they will handle a "little risk." The program is not for families who are comfortable with publication for an unknown father. The risks involved are substantial—Juvenile Court action, trials, involved parents, contested adoptions, and so on. Also, legal situations may change after placement (involved parents may disappear, uninvolved parents may return, and so forth). A prospective family must face these possibilities.

The program does not permit traditional concepts of confidentiality prevalent in adoption. The new parents will know their child's name, for example, often through a medical card. In many situations, the gap between the biological parents and the adoptive parents will not be there. The biological parents may frequently visit the child, though not in the potential adoptive home. An older child may share his new family's name with the biological parents during visits. This poses a threat to many prospective applicants. However, it must be faced; and whether it can be accepted is one determinant as to whether this is a good program for the new family.

Another area of special focus is the disturbing backgrounds from which the children come. In many instances, there is abuse, neglect, abandonment, gross deprivation, mental illness, retardation, and so on. Such situations are often the reason that families initially come to the attention of the state. Foster Care/Adoptive families must be understanding of these situations, even though they see the damaging effect on the child. Also, many of the children come from large families. The prospective adopters must be comforable with this, and accept future contact with siblings or other relatives if indicated.

In terms of procedure, the Foster Care/Adoption program differs from traditional foster care in two significant areas. First, the placement agreement clearly states that the mutual intention of the agency and new family is adoption if the legal matters are resolved. Second, the family has the option of accepting monthly reimbursements for the care of the child, in addition to medical and clothing expenses. Some choose the maximum reimbursement; others elect to provide free foster homes. However, if the child is under state guardianship, the family cannot offer a free foster home.

Besides helping a family determine whether this is the right program for them, the agency must determine whether it is a good program for the child. It often is difficult to ascertain whether the child will become free for adoption. We try to be as clear as possible at the time of referral as to whether the child will become free for adoption. Thus, as much information as possible is needed for discussion with the agency lawyer about the feasibility of Foster Care/Adoptive planning.

SIGNIFICANT POSTPLACEMENT ISSUES

Clearly, by the basic nature of the program families are placed in a difficult position. Will they be the permanent parents to the child they love and wish to make part of their family? Potential loss is a constant threat. Painful reminders are there each time a court hearing occurs or the natural parents express ambivalence about adoption planning. Preparation for this is crucial, particularly in terms of recognizing past losses. For example:

> Susan, one-year-old, has been placed in a Foster Care/Adoptive home after the natural parents relinquished their six-year-old daughter but were not yet able to make such a permanent decision for Susan. They obviously were ambivalent. The adoptive family became increasingly anxious about the possible loss to the point where they considered replacement rather than to continue to suffer emotionally. The agency provided the needed casework services to the family so that the child remained and was eventually adopted by them.

Foster Care/Adoptive families desperately need support during placement. Workers must be honest about any changes in the child's legal situation, but should not precipitously share each new development. The agency must help the family keep their perspective not losing sight of the risk but not emphasizing it.

Because of the tenuousness of the situation, families may begin to feel anger and resentment toward the natural family. These feelings may be fanned if the child is upset by visits with the biological family—for example, refusing to go, regressing after the visit, and so on. The worker must help the adoption applicants recognize and understand the feelings of the biological parents. The worker, too, must be aware of her/his own emotions, and avoid the trap of taking sides.

If it develops that the child must be returned to the biological family, the Foster Care/Adoptive parents have to be helped to mourn. A quick replacement to avoid feelings of pain, would be disastrous, since the family would not have time to resolve their loss.

Group sessions after placement are tremendously beneficial to Foster Care/Adoptive families. They give families a chance to meet others in similar circumstances and with similar concerns, and provide much support during the postplacement period. The group members are encouraged to decide on their own agenda. Issues discussed include visiting with natural parents, facing possible loss of the child, explaining the child's background to him, handling emotional problems of the child and so forth.

CASE ILLUSTRATIONS AND PROBLEMS

Many problems have been encountered in the program. The following case is illustrative.

> Two siblings, David, 2-1/2, and Mary, 6 months, were placed with a Foster Care/Adoptive family upon referal from the State Department. Basic information about the natural family was given. The children were from two of five siblings. Originally there were six in the family, but one child had died of skull fractures resulting from suspected parental abuse. David had experienced extreme deprivation, but had made remarkable progress in a year of foster care. Mary was described as normal and healthy. She was born 6 months after the placement of the other children. The biological parents had free access to the original foster home of these siblings, but had not visited in 6 months. Mary's guardianship hearing had been set for 2 months after the date of placement.
>
> Since this was an emergency placement based on the foster home deterioration, there was not time to provide written material, so it was presented verbally. Immediately after placement, it was learned that Mary had a congenital heart problem. Also, the natural parents had hired a private lawyer to contest the guardianship of Mary, and the trial date was then only a week away. Since these were facts that were not known at placement, the family had to be strong, with the ability to handle the unexpected.
>
> The state finally obtained guardianship (after four continuances) 7 months after the placement with the Foster Care/Adoptive family and 10 months after Mary's initial placement into foster care. This is only the first step toward adoptive rights.

As mentioned earlier, families in the program expect to adopt, thus making a commitment to the child almost before placement. Therefore, they have a right to complete information about a child, so they can make a sound decision. This is an idea often difficult to convey to other social workers; placing children for "adoption with foster parents" is reflected in the adoption process, since families have to be prepared not only for foster care, but for adoption.

Program advantages and disadvantages are illustrated in the cases that follow.

> An eight-month-old boy was referred for Foster Care/Adoption. The natural mother had disappeared 6 weeks prior to the referral, and the alcoholic grandmother could no longer handle the boy in addition to his two older sisters. On the day of placement, the mother reappeared unexpectedly, and after placement, it was discovered that the child was 10 months old, not 8 months, the wrong birth date having been given initially. One year after placement, the biological mother voluntarily relinquished the child feeling secure in the knowledge that the family, to whom the child was attached, would adopt him.

Michael, 18 months old, had experienced material deprivation as an infant and had been in foster care one year. The agency took the case to court on the basis of the mother's limitations and incompetence, but the child was returned to her care. The court did grant the agency 3 months' supervision of mother and child. During this time, the mother began to express a desire to surrender Michael. She was living with a man who would not support any decision she made. She would constantly inform the agency of a different decision. She finally asked to relinquish the child, and a court date was arranged. Whether the mother would follow through on her decision was unknown. It was clear that Michael had to be moved immediately if he was relinquished, but at 18 months, he needed preplacement visiting.

The situation was explained to a waiting Foster Care/Adoptive family willing to assume the risk. The time that the mother was in court was used as a visit to the new family, although they did not know if they would see the child again. It was planned that after the visit Michael would return to the agency either to say goodbye to his mother or to go home with her. The end result was that the mother relinquished the child in court, and we were able to arrange the day so that Michael had an experience with the family before permanently staying. The risk was pressed into a single morning for this family. They had to be extremely strong and flexible to withstand the strain of not knowing whether they would see the child again.

WORKER PROBLEMS

Since this program straddles the two traditional programs of adoption and foster care, philosophical difficulties are sometimes encountered. The question arises as to whether the agency is trying to "snatch" a child from his biological parents and therefore to undermine any attempt at rehabilitation. This is one reason a determination must be made at the outset that rehabilitation has been attempted unsuccessfully and that the problems appear chronic, and thus adoption seems to be in the best interests of the child. Unless all the workers involved are convinced of this they may work against each other. Rehabilitation can happen even in cases that appear to be the most difficult—hence the risk.

The following illustrates a breakdown in worker cooperation.

The worker for the Foster Care/Adoptive family and the worker for the biological parents worked against each other in a case involving a retarded mother. She was barely able to function on her own, could not provide any parenting to her two children, and was not able to protect her children from her friends who physically abused

> them. The children were placed with a Foster Care/Adoptive family, and evidence for a legal case was being gathered. After placement the mother wanted to visit the children, and this was arranged. Her worker insisted upon reminding her of visits, driving her to and from the visits, and so on. The Foster Care/Adoption worker thought that the mother had every right to visit but that she must do it on her own; otherwise the legal case, documenting her incompetence, would be weakened. The mother's worker felt that it would be cruel to expect the mother to visit on her own.

On occasion, the worker for the biological parents must be prepared to testify against her clients. Therefore, the worker must be firmly convinced that adoption is the best plan for the child and must be able to support that belief in whatever way is legally necessary.

STATISTICS

Since the beginning of the program in 1973 to the date of this writing, the agency has placed seventeen children with fifteen families (two sibling groups). Two other Foster Care/Adoption situations were resolved prior to placement (the legal resolution was not known at the time the families were approached about the children). Seven conversions to adoption had occurred by the end of 1974. Termination of parental rights was achieved by means of trial, default, and voluntary consent. Thus far a majority served have been in the infancy and preschool age ranges, although the program has not been restricted in age range. Most of the children have been boys. Two were black infants and several were minority nationalities, such as Mexican and Puerto Rican. All were ostensibly healthy physically, but the majority had emotional disturbances due to early experiences. Work on the remaining Foster Care/Adoption cases continues. To date, no child has been replaced or returned to the natural families.

20

ADOPTION OF REAL CHILDREN: EXCERPTS

JOAN SHIREMAN AND KENNETH W. WATSON

In a demonstration project of the Chicago Child Care Society, adoptive applicants were given the major responsibility for choosing the child they wished to adopt from among those waiting in the agency's foster homes. The new service proved effective for placing these children.

Probably the most difficult and persistent problem in adoption today is placing children for whom homes were not found in early infancy. In practice, current adoption procedures too often lead to seeking a child to match an applicant's expectations. Children who do not meet these expectations are excluded. In time they become practically unadoptable because of their age and their history of moves in foster care. Their future is bleak.

Finding homes for hard-to-place children has long been a primary concern of the adoption program of the Chicago Child Care Society (CCCS)—a voluntary, nonsectarian, multiple-service child care agency. As part of the agency's effort to improve its service, a team of workers developed a new approach to adoption. The essential characteristics of this approach were (1) engaging in work only with families interested in actual children awaiting homes, and (2) whenever possible, shifting responsibility for decision-making to the applicants. In practice, agency workers showed photographs and presented detailed information about specific children to adoptive applicants. Any applicant interested in one of these children then explored with the worker the feasibility of bringing this child into his family.

A four-month demonstration project indicated that the new service was effective in finding homes for some hard-to-place children. It has also evoked a generally enthusiastic response from applicants, aroused much interest throughout the region, and brought up many vital issues that should be examined. The authors believe that the service is well worth further development and trial in other settings.

ADOPTION PROBLEMS

The CCCS adoption department has always been considered innovative. Since 1955 it has been committed to finding homes for black children. It was among the first to place black children in white homes and to place children with single persons. These new ideas had caused slow changes in the CCCS adoption process, which was not unlike the process in many other agencies. Applicants first discussed their interest and the type of child they wanted in a comprehensive telephone interview with the worker. If their requests were appropriate, they were invited to come to the agency for an intake interview. A series of interviews followed as the home was studied. When the home was approved, a decision was made about the type of child to be placed. If there was such a child waiting in the CCCS preadoptive foster care program, he was placed. If there was no such waiting child and the family considered adopting only a certain type of child, the worker sought a child in other agencies' caseloads, through formal and informal exchange programs. Thus some families waited while the worker searched for the right child, yet other children waited in foster homes.

Several factors precipitated a decision to review the conceptual basis of this adoption process: (1) the large number of children for whom homes could not be found, (2) adoptive parents' comments about delays in service and their sense of helplessness during the study period, (3) caseworkers' discomfort about the judgmental aspects of the study, (4) the consistent failure of research to demonstrate an association between subtle indicators of poor parent potential and later outcome, and (5) the theoretical conflict between matching a child to an applicant's fantasy and expecting the applicant to be a parent to a real child.

Five premises that should underlie adoption were developed:

(1) Within our society the family is the best-known milieu for rearing children—hopefully the family into which a child is born, but if

that cannot be, then a substitute one that provides permanence and security, preferably through legal adoption.

(2) It is the adoption agencies' responsibility to find adequate homes for all children who need them.

(3) An adoption agency best fulfills this responsibility by providing a service that facilitates bringing together children who need homes and families interested in adoption.

(4) Most families that come to an agency for adoption do not have serious pathological problems and have at least an average capacity to become adoptive parents.

(5) Given accurate and adequate information, most people are better able to make their own important life decisions than to have others make them.

The new adoption service was developed on the basis of these concepts. It focused on serving children currently needing homes and stressed applicants' ability to make decisions.

The existing adoption department was left relatively untouched, so that the effectiveness of the new and the more traditional processes might be compared. The team selected to develop and work the demonstration project consisted of the agency's director of foster care and adoption services, the CCCS research director, a caseworker working primarily in foster care, and a relatively new worker in the adoption department.

NEW TECHNIQUES

The service developed by this team differed in two essential ways from the agency's existing adoption program. First, the focus was on finding homes for children already known to the agency and awaiting adoption. As each aspect of the project was developed, it was tested with the question, "Will this benefit the waiting children?" Second, the responsibility for decision-making was allocated, whenever possible, to the applicants rather than the workers. It became the applicants' responsibility to decide whether they were interested in one of the children available for adoption, whether they wished to work with the agency toward adoption, with which worker they wished to explore adoption, and which child they were interested in adopting. They then considered with the worker the factors involved in taking the specific child into their home.

This shift in responsibility necessarily involved changes in practice. Every applicant whose inquiry was referred to the project was invited to come to the agency. If his time permitted, he came to a scheduled group meeting, otherwise for and individual interview. No preliminary screening was done. It was felt that acquainting applicants with needs of waiting children might help them think further about the kinds of children they were capable of adopting. Whether or not the applicants could accept any of the available children, the message about the needs of real children would be reaching a wider public.

To make the children as real as possible, the agency kept an album containing recent photographs of all its waiting children and of some children available through referral from other agencies. At the initial meeting workers showed pictures of a few typical children to the applicants, explained the plan of working only toward the placement of waiting children, outlined the process, and answered questions. Applicants who wished to pursue adoption through CCCS could make an appointment for an individual meeting with the project worker they chose from those attending the group meeting. Applicants who felt they could not accept one of the waiting children were referred to another agency.

Since every applicant was assumed to have an average capacity to be a parent, unless evidence of unusual behavior was immediately observable, almost all applicants who set up an individual interview to discuss adoption further were free to look at the photo album during their interview. At that time most selected a child by asking questions about the children pictured. In response to their queries, all known information that was not confidential was given. Once selected, a child was reserved for the particular applicant as long as he was seriously working with the agency toward the child's adoption.

In that interview and as many subsequent interviews as necessary, worker and applicant discussed the child's needs, his probable impact on the family, and how the family might cope with his addition to their family unit. A mutual evaluation of the wisdom of the adoption of a given child by a given family replaced the agency's evaluation of the family in the ongoing adoption program. In this evaluation process many traditionally explored areas were considered, but always in relation to the specific child. Either agency or client had the option of deciding not to proceed, or the family could later change its mind about a given child when the reality of the situation became more apparent.

Placement occurred as soon as worker and family were comfortable with both the idea of adoption and the family's choice of child, legal requirements were completed and the child was ready to be placed. Placement procedures were based on the child's needs, because the adoptive parent already knew much about the child and had been talking about him with the agency for some time.

EVALUATION PLAN

After four months' operation the project was evaluated. The number of waiting children who were actually placed in the project was compared with placements in the ongoing adoption program, during the same period and during the same four months a year before. To discover whether the new approach discouraged or encouraged applicants, each applicant's progress from intake to termination or service was recorded for both the project and the department. After termination, each project applicant was asked for his opinion about his experience with the agency. Team members' ideas about the strengths and weaknesses of the new approach were also recorded.

Applicants to whom the new service was offered were selected on a random basis. Inquiries about a first adoption from CCCS were randomly assigned from letters or the switchboard to the project or the department, in proportion to the intake needs of the applicants. Thus, 113 families were assigned to the project and 85 to the department. When the project results were first presented to the adoption staff as a whole, another source of intake was discovered. The department was working with twenty-three additional families who had made initial telephone inquiries directly to one of the department workers. These calls were, therefore, never recorded as inquiries at the switchboard and did not become part of the pool from which families were randomly assigned.

Of the randomly assigned families, about half were white couples asking about adopting white infants. Approximately 20 percent were black couples requesting black children. Most of the remainder were white families wishing to adopt transracially; the project had a higher proportion of those interested in a part-black child. The twenty-three families who contacted the department directly were different; there were fifteen black and four white couples interested in a black child and four white couples interested in a mixed nonblack child.

These families, then, comprised the intake for a four-month period. All project placements were, of course, with couples in this group. However, all but one of the departmental placements during the period were with couples who had applied earlier. There is not reason to think that the group of earlier applicants differed appreciably from those applying in this period.

CONCLUSIONS

The CCCS adoption project was a four-month demonstration to see whether adoption service to hard-to-place children could be improved by a process based on applicants' interest in adopting children who were waiting and their assumption of greater responsibility in decision-making.

The major fingings were as follows:

(1) Although the project failed to place the most difficult waiting children, it placed a number of older children during a period when the department placed none in that age group. It also made more transracial placements. It did not facilitate adoption of easily placed infants.

(2) Project placements were made more quickly and were more economical of workers' time. In proportion to available staff hours, the project placed one-and-a-half times as many children as the department.

(3) Project families resembled closely those served by the department, and project placements gave no indication of being less successful than the others.

(4) The majority of applicants liked the process. Restricting adoption to waiting children caused no evident increase in applicant loss. Even if applicants could not adopt a child, they respected the agency's commitment to waiting children. The majority also expressed satisfaction about their decision-making responsibility. A few expanded their ideas so that they were able to adopt one of the children needing a home.

(5) Project workers were enthusiastic about the new process and deeply committed to it.

Comparison of project and departmental service is clouded by the fact that some applicants were not randomly assigned to the two services. Because the initial telephone inquiries to specific departmental workers were not included in the pool of applicants, the department served a higher proportion of black families than the project. Most of these inquiries were from families referred by friends of the agency's adoptive parents, or screened by the city's adoption information service. It seems probable that a high proportion of them might have been somewhat ready to accept one of the waiting children. Had the comparison been based on completely random sample selection, the project's efficiency and effectiveness might have been even more marked.

From both the applicant's and the worker's points of view, the project process offers substantial possibilities for facilitating adoption procedures. The shift of responsibilities for the child's selection from worker to applicant shows that the applicant was treated as a mature, functioning individual. The change then was from meeting the needs of the client-applicant to meeting the needs of the client-child—a move consistent with current child welfare practices.

Numerous facets of the approach need further thought and experimentation. For example, intriguing differences in the decision-making process were observed. Some applicants seemed to enjoy going through the large numbers of pictures presented, returning to a few, and gradually making their choice. Others seemed overwhelmed by the numbers. A few expressed remorse about the children they rejected. Learning to tailor this process to the applicant's maximum ease and the children's maximum benefit is a next step.

The selection process was imperfect in other ways too. Snapshots are a weak medium for presenting children. They emphasize appearance, a minor aspect to most would-be parents. Advantages of videotape and other devices might be explored. Also, ways might be sought to retain the benefits of the active participation by applicants provided by perusal of the album. Evaluation of procedures would have been more meaningful had there been a greater variety of children. For example, there were few handicapped children among those in the foster homes at the time of the project. Thus, how effective this method may be in finding homes for these children is not known.

New approaches are vital to meet the needs of children awaiting adoptive homes. This project tested one such approach and found it to be generally popular with applicants, and helpful in placing some children waiting for adoptive homes. It would seem valuable now to test the approach in other settings, build on its findings, and seek to resolve the questions and concerns it has raised. Surely it is through careful formulation of underlying ideas, development of a practice method, tests, evaluation, and refinement of the method that we will discover the most effective way to find good adoptive homes for all waiting children.

ABOUT THE EDITORS

SALLIE R. CHURCHILL is professor of Social Work and coordinator of the Children and Youth Concentration at The University of Michigan School of Social Work.

BONNIE CARLSON teaches social welfare at the State University of New York at Albany, and has taught courses of child development and the family at the University of Michigan. She has also done research on battered women and dual-career families.

LYNN NYBELL is an associate of the Continuing Education Program in the Human Services of The University of Michigan School of Social Work. She coordinated the materials development efforts of Project CRAFT.